THINK
BIG

By Dick Beals

D1545417

Cover design: Don Manning, Manning and Associates
San Diego
Original Illustration — Jim Wainwright

ISBN 0-9632343-0-7

Thank You...

If Don and Irene Manning hadn't kept insisting that I write THINK BIG, I'd still be just talking about it.

Linda Chester's excellent critique caused me to rewrite the manuscript into its present form. And the constructive comments from test market readers Sharon Singleton, Forrest Owen and Dorothy Honnen made it even better.

Don Manning designed the cover, utilizing the original illustration by Jim Wainwright. Don's staff also pieced together photos from 60 years back to create all those picture pages.

The final touch came from Dr. Don Yates, at Miles. His editing put the icing on the cake.

Again, thank you all.

T H I N K
BIG

CONTENTS

1
Growing Up Small

"Bonanza-niner-one-six-one-Quebec, cleared for *immediate* takeoff, Lear just inside the outer marker," came the tower chief at Palomar Airport.

"Six-one-Quebec, we're rolling," I replied.

Anticipating the order, I had gone almost to full power before he finished the sentence. That "made" the Lear jet pilot's day in line behind me. He didn't want a go-around at this point all because some slowpoke was still on the runway.

Climbing through 800 feet, I am soon being swallowed by the low clouds and fog so common along the southern California coast, even in early October. I raise the gear, ease the power back to a cruise-climb setting, inch my seat back a notch, and focus every ounce of my concentration on the instruments.

"Six-one-Quebec, contact Departure on 125.6, and enjoy the game."

"Thank you, that's 125.6. See you Sunday." Now how did they know where I was going? "Departure, Bonanza-niner-one-six-one-Quebec with you, climbing to 10,000."

"Six-one-Quebec, roger, report reaching ten."

Flight Service told me the tops were around 3,500 feet, and going through 3,000 the darkness and gloom inside the clouds started to brighten slowly. Airplane drivers see a lot of fantastic sights. But one that never failed to thrill me was climbing through that last hazy veil of clouds and popping up into the blinding sunshine. Beneath that blanket of pure, soft whiteness is all the gloom and dampness. But on top . . . *heaven*. Palomar Mountain and the Cuyamacas 60 miles to the east poked their heads and shoulders through the cloud deck. Ahead, the mountains north of the Los Angeles basin were in view 125 miles away. And it was clear all the way to Palo Alto, with a warm sunny, Indian summer forecast for the Purdue-Stanford game.

Just as the Oceanside VOR flicked from TO to FROM on my #1 Nav, the voice in my headset said, "Six-one-Quebec, contact Coast Approach on 124.1. Enjoy the game, Speedy."

"Six-one-Quebec, 124.1, Plop-plop-fizz-fizz."

How word gets around an airport! I had casually mentioned to the youngster topping off my tanks that I was headed up to the Bay area for the Purdue-Stanford game. Now all the world knew it.

The call from Purdue's athletic director, Red Mackey, back in West Lafayette, had come from out of the blue. "Hey there, little red head, how you-all doin'?''

If I had red hair, then the ex-football star at Purdue had flaming hair. "I'm fine, overworked and not playing enough golf. What's up?''

"How's the new ad agency doing?''

"It's fine, but I *told* you I'm overworked, and not playing enough golf.''

"Still flying your airplane?''

"Of course.''

"Can you make it up to Palo Alto for our game? I'm saving you a seat in the press box.''

"Oh, you bet. But can I get a reservation up there at this late date?''

"Not to worry. I'll put you on our team list.'' And then he started to laugh so hard he nearly dropped the phone.

"What's so funny?''

"I can just see the hotel clerk when you check in and he sees your name on our team list. You, barely able to see over the top of the front desk, and this poor clerk trying to figure out what position you're going to play. Oh, that's funny. I can't wait.''

"Hey pal, can't you put me on your VIP list or something?''

"OK, I'll think of something,'' he said, still chuckling. "See you Friday.''

Red Mackey and I were old friends and I knew he meant no harm by making a joke of my size, or lack of size. At only 4'6'', you run into a lot of crude people, but you learn to ignore them, eventually, swallowing a lot of hurt feelings. Eventually, you learn that a quick smile disarms most of them, even the bullies, who think you're a minority, and figure you're an easy target.

People don't deserve to be made fun of for altering a car so they can drive it, but they are. Extending the pedals a few inches and sitting on a cushion is just being practical.

The reactions of bystanders and airport personnel when I climb out of my airplane, alone, have been hilarious. They're dying to know what ingenious device allows me to reach everything and see out.

I'm not the only pilot that sits on a cushion. Mine are thicker and I also use one at my back. But rudder pedals aren't positioned for folks 4'6'' (even with two cushions), so I designed a device that straps onto my shoes, and extends the soles of my shoes another 4''—kind of like roller skates with a solid platform instead of the wheels. This way I can fly any airplane I want to, even the Lear jet that was on my tail as I was departing Palomar Airport.

But, of course, the big thrill is when my childlike voice comes booming into an FAA control tower. Around my home base, I'm well known. They know I do cartoon voices and commercials for a living, and own an ad agency. And, thanks to an article in the local papers, when I moved to the Escondido area, people learned I was the voice of Speedy Alka-Seltzer. But away from those friendly skies, the reactions were funny. Fully aware of the problem, I tried to sound as professional as possible.

Such was the case this day as San Jose slid under my wings and Oakland Center handed me off to Palo Alto Tower. In my most professional sounding voice I said, "Palo Alto Tower, Bonanza-niner-one-six-one-Quebec, ten south landing, with the numbers."

"Six-one-Quebec, roger, report downwind."

The small airport next to the Bay was wide open, so I landed, got off the active, contacted Ground Control, and was directed to Transient Parking. As I was taxiing past the tower, I glanced up, and there were four controllers, all with binoculars, watching my every move. Sensing what was coming, I decided to look busy and ignore them. But not the men in the tower. One grabbed the mike and said with great authority, "Six-one-Quebec, Palo Alto Tower requests the age of the pilot."

I was so pleased that I had even found their little airport, I pushed the mike button and responded, "Palo Alto Tower, the pilot first voted for Thomas E. Dewey."

The binoculars went down, looks were exchanged, shoulders shrugged, then up came the binoculars, up came the mike, and the tower chief asked, "Six-one-Quebec, who the hell is Thomas E. Dewey?"

* * *

I wasn't always small. When the stork unloaded me in 1927, I weighed in at 9½ pounds. I was my parents' dream of the big, strong athlete . . . cheering crowds and all that stuff. My mother often said, "I could just hear the crowds yelling, 'Yea Dick, yea Dick!'" Actually I was named after Richard Henry Lee, one of the signers of the Constitution and an ancestor on my mother's side. She was a Lee, so Richard Lee Beals was hung on me that March 16 in a small apartment in Detroit.

She was right on two counts. I was going to be athletically inclined and well coordinated, and crowds would be cheering . . . but only because I was the cheerleader. They wouldn't be yelling, "Yea Dick," either.

At a year old, I wasn't getting much bigger. They were beginning to realize they were faced with bringing up a child that would be small—really small—and they didn't have the slightest idea of how to handle it. Unfortunately, neither did

3

medical science, then or now for that matter. But my parents were Christian Scientists, and they knew down deep that if I was to be successful at anything, anything at all, they were going to need all the spiritual help they could get.

In 1930 we moved to the lovely residential community of Birmingham, 15 miles northwest of Detroit. Our home was two blocks from Pierce School, and in '32 I started kindergarten. By then my parents had some idea of what they had on their hands. At two-and-one-half years old I sang a solo at my grandmother's church in Detroit. I must have liked being the center of attention. But even at that age I remember one thing vividly . . . when my mother said to do something, I did it. No questions asked. "Don't have to be coaxed," she would say.

Then something happened that affected my life more than anything else. The high school football field was built on the outskirts of town adjacent to where I attended school. After kindergarten class one day I wandered over to see what was going on.

I had never seen a football uniform before or a football. I guess because I was small and cute and never what you'd call shy, one of the players started tossing the football to me. Another player taught me how to catch this huge football and how to run with it, and suddenly I was the center of attention. Which, of course, I loved. The coach, Mr. Robinson, noticed this and let me hold his clipboard, hold his stopwatch, blow his whistle when he pointed at me and all kinds of "important" assignments. I was hooked. I was there for every practice.

To top it all off he suggested to the team that I be named official mascot of the Baldwin High School football team. I was unanimously elected. This meant I was allowed in the locker room, the captain would carry me into the stadium on his shoulders, I sat on the bench, took towels to my heroes, saw bones broken and noses bleed and, more importantly, was in the locker room after the game when they won or when they lost. I saw my heroes laugh and yell when they won and cry when they lost. And I laughed and yelled. And I cried and cried. For a kid only five years old and really small, this was the most powerful and valuable education I ever could have received. It was deeply imbedded forever.

I not only learned the game of football and had real heroes, but I learned that size didn't mean a thing, and from that moment on I never saw myself as small. I saw only the task or the challenge. I knew that what counted was discipline and hard work and dedication to that task. Most important though was that tremendous need to win. From then on, in everything I did, I had to win. From then on, it was THINK BIG.

4

My big brother Terry, about three years older, was a bit small for his age and I was tiny. No matter what the sport, the two of us took on the neighborhood. Football, basketball, hockey, baseball, no matter. With the football I absorbed at high school practice everyday and knowing all our plays and techniques, Terry and I put this knowledge into good use in our neighborhood backyard games. We would figure out a way to win and did. I lived and breathed sports, and in those depression days that's all we had to do. We always had a radio. After school Terry and I listened to Little Orphan Annie, Buck Rogers, Jack Armstrong and Tom Mix, as long as we kept the volume down so as not to wake up our new little brother, Bob. After dinner, we were allowed up to hear Amos & Andy and The Lone Ranger; then at 8 p.m. it was "jammy" time. If I was hooked on sports I was also hooked on radio.

Those early competitive experiences set the stage for the direction my life was going to take. Winning meant survival. I was going to have to compete for everything I ever did. Nothing was going to be handed to me.

The road to performing was beginning to take shape. Football provided the first big jump. The high school cheerleaders thought it would be cute if "Red," that's me, would lead cheers. So they taught me a basic cheer and picked a moment in the big game for my debut. You can imagine what that did to me and for me. Center of attention, spotlight, the audience following my every move, the power, the applause. Of course you know how the crowd reacted. They yelled their tonsils out.

The high school immediately retired their mascot and elected me to the varsity cheerleading squad. I was almost seven.

The road to performing moved onward and upward. My mother was the positive thinker in the family. She knew that if I was ever to be successful, it would be in performing. Despite the cold hard facts: the depression, hard times, just a housewife . . . she kept the faith. Soon, God led us to open doors of opportunity.

We were leaving the J. L. Hudson Company in downtown Detroit one summer day, and she ran into an old high school friend. His name was Dave Andrews and they had been classmates at Northwestern High School some 18 years earlier. They exchanged pleasantries and then Dave noticed me. I was eight and, as taught for years, was barely to be seen and not heard.

"Hi there, young man," he said, "what's your name?"

"Dick, Mr. Andrews," I answered politely.

"How old is he, Dorothy, about four?"

"No, he's eight."

He really looked me over. Then he started asking me questions—what grade was I in, what school, favorite subjects. "Dorothy, I'm a director at Jam Handy Picture Studios, and I could really use him. It wouldn't pay much, but it would surely help us out. How about it?"

"Help you out how?"

"We do a lot of commercials for dealer showrooms, and they like to have children in them. But try to get a four-year-old to do what you tell them. Dick looks four but has an eight-year-old's intelligence. That would really help us."

"Well, let me talk it over with my husband."

Phone numbers and addresses were exchanged and we went home. If it was discussed further, it was in private. I never heard another word about it.

Then my mother told me one morning as I got up for school that I wasn't going to school but was going to Jam Handy.

After breakfast I was dressed in my best pants and best shirt and put into the car—and down to Detroit we went. The instructions were not too short and not too sweet. "Now pay attention and do what you're told, you understand?"

I nodded. "Will there be an audience?"

"No, you will be in a studio."

"Whatever that is," I thought.

The 30-minute drive was a continuous dialog of dos and don'ts. I was glad to get there.

We were ushered into this big barn of a place with lights all over and a big camera and important-looking people standing around. Mr. Andrews (that's what I was told to call him . . . about 20 times) took me to a room where a man put makeup on me, which I didn't like then and still don't. Then I was taken back to the set, which was a living room scene featuring a big, new, Magnavox console radio. I was to sit on the floor at my "parents'" feet with an Airedale and just look cute. The dog didn't like sitting there, so they nailed a wire into the carpet and hooked it onto his collar. That didn't work either, so I braved all kinds of possible reprisals going home and whispered to Mr. Andrews that I'd like to talk to him.

"Yes, Dick, what is it."

"If it's OK, I think I can hold onto the dog until you're ready, then pet him during the time when we're supposed to act. He'll be OK, I promise. We're friends now."

"OK, let's try it." And he went back to the crew and told them what he was going to do; the guy came in and undid the wire and what's-his-name was all mine. It never occurred to me the dog probably outweighed me. I knew he could outrun me.

What I never counted on was how many times we had to shoot one simple scene. It took hours. Different angles, closeups, long shots, two-shots, dog shots, kid shots. But bless that big dog . . . his mother must have talked to him all the way to the studio, too. He did a good job.

By mid-afternoon the shooting day was over. I said goodbye and shook hands with everyone as I had been instructed to do, many times. I saw my mother get a check from the secretary, and we drove home.

Almost seven hours on the set. The check was for $2. But a depression was going on and that was a lot of money for a kid to make. All I had to do was sit around, hold a dog and look cute. You call that work? Yes . . . I do. Especially for an eight-year-old. It was a long day.

The next job came from Wilding Studios and was more demanding and much more painful. I was about to learn more about the magic of film-making. I was to be a street urchin, dressed in tattered clothes with makeup that dirtied my face. The film was a commercial for a brand new thing called a "supermarket."

"Now Dickie," began the director as if he were talking to a four-year-old.

"I prefer Dick, sir."

"Of course, Dick. Now uh, uh, Dick, do you know what a street urchin is?"

"Yes, sir. I looked it up in the dictionary this morning."

"Uh, yeah, the dictionary. Well, uh, anyway a street urchin is not necessarily a bad child but maybe mischievous. Now we want you to push and bump your way through the women shopping at the fresh fruit counter, grab as many strawberries as you can, stuff them in your mouth, eat them and run for the door." And patting me on top of the head, he said, "Now then, uh, uh, Dick, do we think we can do that, just for me?"

"Yes . . . SIR!!" Would I ever be big enough that people would cease treating me like a three-year-old? We rehearsed it a few times. I guess my "pushes and bumps" were a little too pushy and bumpy and the "shoppers" complained to the management.

"Now, Dickie . . ." My head snapped up sharply. "Uh, I mean, Dick, uh, we want this urchin to be nicer or a little more polite. Do you understand . . . polite?"

"Yes, sir. I'll work my way into the strawberry area with the same motions but with less contact."

"Oh, Dick, that will be just marvelous," and he flitted away gracefully.

Now the real thing. In came the produce that would have wilted or sagged under the hot lights. I kept my eye on the strawberries. As they were arranging them, I picked out the exact berries that I would stuff in my mouth. There was time to do extra dry runs, practice a few little added moves like at the last second reaching back as far as I could and grabbing one extra berry and jamming it, politely, of course, into my bulging mouth. The big moment arrived as soon as the last berry was placed. With all that heat, they had to move quickly. Places, action.

My extra rehearsing paid off. The last strawberry was in place and I started to chew like mad without choking. But I couldn't chew. The strawberries were frozen solid. But knowing I must chew or ruin the scene I chewed. I can still feel the pain today. Aching teeth, cheeks, gums, lips, throat and whatever. By the time I was out of the shot it was down the hatch. What an ordeal.

"Cut, cut!" screamed the director. "OK, not bad. I have just a few things." He proceeded to correct minor things here and there, until he got to the strawberry kid. "Now, could we have our nice little street urchin stuff a few more strawberries in his mouth." It wasn't a question.

"Yes, sir, I'll try." I was thinking that the lights would be melting the strawberries and it would be no sweat. No such luck. They were already bringing in more frozen ones.

Four takes later, four, we got it. To me it didn't make any difference. My cheeks, mouth, gums and throat were numb. My teeth weren't, though. They just ached and ached. A mouthful of hot water finally helped.

At Ross Roy Studios they needed some stills of a kid taking a clock apart, or rather a kid trying to put the thing back together. Properly. And failing. That was type casting if I ever saw it. How did they know I was an expert at doing just that?

We never got any advance warning that a work call was imminent. Sometimes it came in at 8:30 a.m. for a noon session. Of course, I would be in school. For one job the director wanted me to be dressed in school clothes, which wasn't a problem because that was what I was wearing in my seventh-grade class. But you know mothers. They want their little darlings to look nicely dressed. The problem was that my younger brother Bob, who was now in the first grade, wore the same size clothes as I did and it was his week to wear the nice, new corduroy knickers. I had on the older pair.

My mother wasn't one to rest on ceremony. She marched into my classroom, talked quietly to the teacher, spotted me quickly and waved me out of the classroom.

"Where are we going?"

"Down to Bob's room and change pants."

"Why?"

"Jam Handy wants you."

Into Bob's classroom we marched. She talked to the teacher, motioned Bob into the cloakroom and despite Bob's protestations we changed pants. Shy little Bob emerged red-faced to find 30 pairs of eyes staring at him trying to figure out what he had done wrong.

I was lucky. I got to leave town.

And speaking of leaving town, the idea of trying Hollywood came up at the dinner table one night. It had all started when the manager of the Birmingham Theater, Howard Holla, took me to Detroit to meet Spanky McFarlin, the star of Our Gang Comedy. He was on a personal appearance tour. I met him backstage at the Michigan Theater, got his autograph, chatted, watched him perform and came home. Howard Holla saw my potential and was trying to get my parents to let him be my agent. He suggested that he send my picture to Hal Roach Studios in Hollywood.

"What good would that do?" my dad asked my mother, after much thought.

"It could do a lot of good. Mr. Holla thinks they would use him if they knew about him."

"But we don't have a decent picture of him. And I don't have $10 to have a pro do it."

"Then we'll take our own." Mother never argued with my dad in front of us or anyone.

"But what if they do like the photo? What if they would offer him a job? Do you expect me to just give up my job and move to Hollywood and start looking for a job out there?" he asked as if his sip of coffee had been sour.

And then came the answer that will ring in my ears forever.

"WE WILL GO IF THEY CALL! You'll find something."

End of discussion.

We sent a photo taken in our backyard with a Kodak box camera, accompanied by a nice note in my mother's best handwriting on her best notepaper. They never called. But she was right. If I could have had a shot at Hollywood at that time I would have been a busy young actor. Dad wouldn't have needed a job though he would have found one.

So it was an occasional acting job in Detroit through grade school and junior high school. Then World War II brought an end to my movie-making. The Jam Handys of the world made war training films. My performing exploits were limited to cheerleading and school plays and variety shows.

While my classmates were growing by leaps and bounds, I was slowly inching my way to almost 3½ feet tall and getting more and more discouraged. Doctors tried shooting me full of something or other but nothing worked.

Due to changes in our family life my interest in school waned, grades dropped and chances for a college life came to seem beyond reach.

Terry was now a navy fighter pilot, dad was working overtime in a new and bigger job at General Motors, Bob was six years younger but much taller, which didn't help my self-esteem much. Mother was teaching art classes in our home every day but then became ill and required extensive surgery. The kid in the spotlight was suddenly all alone in the corner feeling no one cared what he did . . . so he didn't either.

All my high school teachers, seeing me drop from A's to C's, and knowing my parents quite well, tried to inspire me by using reverse psychology. They told me I wasn't smart enough to go to college. Like a jerk, I believed them.

In 1932, Dick was named mascot of the Baldwin High School varsity football team. This picture appeared in the 1936 Football Program for the Thanksgiving Day game between traditional rivals Royal Oak and Birmingham.

(At right) In 1934, at age seven, Dick's second film appearance, as a street urchin in a new fangled thing called a super market. He learned, the painful way, that frozen strawberries are difficult to chew.

(Below) His first encounter with a still photo session, Ross Roy Studios, Detroit.

(Below right) The Mascot, at age eight, is promoted to Varsity Cheerleader, seen here leading his first cheer, a rousing "Maroon and White".

(Above)12 year old Dick Beals with "Our Gang Comedy" star, Spanky McFarland, backstage at the Michigan Theater, Detroit. "I still have that autograph," reports Dick, 53 years later.

Age 11, 6th grade, Dick poses with referees prior to football game. At right, Herman Everhardst, former star halfback at University of Michigan.

(Above right) "Slugger", prize winning photograph by Charles Beals, Dick's dad. At age 13, his hopes of becoming the Detroit Tiger's next slugger begin to fade.

(Below) "Flank Attack", another prize winning photo by Dick's dad. The dog is Biffy, the family's wire haired terrier, Dick is 15.

(Below right) Dick in his cap and gown, "Class of 1944", Baldwin High School, Birmingham, Michigan. Photo taken by his dad.

2
Angel Voices Open New Doors

If being lost means having no idea where you are going, then I was lost. The only time I would wake up would be when I accidentally banged my head on a door knob. With college out of sight, I drifted along. The only things that interested me were school variety shows, cheerleading, math and summer jobs. Especially one summer job. That was to get my mind thinking in a new direction, one that would pay off big. God had directed his Angel Voices to deliver a wakeup call.

A family friend heard I was looking for a summer job so he took me down to the Book Cadillac Hotel in Detroit and introduced me to the manager. He gave me a job as page boy. It was a six-day-a-week job, minimal salary and all the tips I could earn.

It was one heck of a learning experience with one tremendous perk. Four major league baseball teams stayed at the Book: the Yankees, the Red Sox, the Philadelphia Athletics and the Washington Senators. Also frequenting the hotel was the ex-Tiger great Harry Heilmann, the Detroit Tiger announcer.

The players took me out to the ballpark, I sat on the bench, and actually worked out at second base with Bobby Doerr, the Boston star. Harry Heilmann, though, was the key. He invited me out to the ballpark, took me into the locker rooms, and introduced me to the greatest names in baseball, Bill Dickey, Joe Gordon, Connie Mack, Charlie Keller, Early Wynn, Mickey Vernon and George Metkovich.

Then he took me into his broadcast booth and let me watch him do a few innings before I had to rush back to work. Every time he saw me wandering through the lobby paging someone he invited me to go out with him. And soon I was hooked, but good. There was no doubt in my mind. I wanted to be around sports and I wanted to be a sports announcer.

As much money as I made that summer, college was still beyond reach. I knew my grades were too poor to even consider it. But the dream stayed there.

My senior year was uneventful. I did go out for baseball. The coach was new and he thought it would be funny to have someone try to pitch to me. I got in one game, crouched way down, but their pitcher threw blooper pitches and the stupid ump called me out on strikes. (I didn't care for his seeing-eye dog.)

With my brother Terry in the audience, resplendent in his

Navy uniform with ensign bars and wings gleaming, I graduated, somehow. Dad got me a job in the mail room at the General Motors plant in Pontiac. Within a year I had progressed from mail room, to a typing job, to bigger typing jobs, and was hauling down $135 a month. I was saving every cent, living at home and paying $10 a week for room and board.

If there is one thing I've learned through the years it is this. Change won't come into your life until deep down you are ready for it. Ready for it mentally. You may not be aware that you are thinking change. But in your subconscious you are. Right about then I must have been thinking change or betterment or moving onward and upward. Because it was about then that an Angel Voice descended into my life and was about to turn my life around.

It was March, 1945. A student from Albion College started sitting right behind me in this huge office. During dull moments she and I would chat about nothing in particular, but one day it got around to college.

"Dick, I can't figure out why you're here and not in college. It just doesn't make sense."

I gave her my standard spiel. "Oh, my grades aren't that good. My teachers told me I wouldn't stand a chance . . . that I'd have to take courses I couldn't pass and, well . . . "

"What do you want to do?"

"Sports announcer, radio, sing, stuff like that."

"Why don't you major in that then?"

"Major in what?" I asked, thinking it was a joke.

"Radio, broadcasting, sports announcing, sports writing. You know a lot about sports. You could certainly learn to write about it. You'd be good."

The sales pitch continued, day after day. But with only about $1,200 saved, and poor grades! Naw.

"Where would you like to go to school if you could?" the campaign continued.

"Michigan State. My brother was going there before he joined the Navy V-5 program. He had me up for a weekend once and I stayed in his dorm and saw a basketball game. It's real neat."

"Do they have a radio curriculum?" She knew darn well they did.

"I don't know."

"Do you know anyone in radio that could tell you? Like, how about Ty Tyson? You said you met him in the Tiger locker room one day. Call him."

"Oh, he wouldn't remember me."

"He might. Call him and ask for an appointment. I'll bet he'd love to help you."

Ty Tyson was a radio pioneer. He did the very first radio broadcast of a baseball game in 1924, over what is now WWJ. He was my hero. With a trembling voice, I called him. "Yes, of course I remember you. You were with Harry Heilmann. What can I do for you?"

"Well," I stammered, "could I come down and see you. I need some advice on a few things."

"What sort of 'things,' son?"

"Well, uh, like college and a radio career and what I should do, and things like that."

"Well, OK," he sighed, figuring he just couldn't say no. I could hear him leafing through some pages. "It's a little close but how about tomorrow morning at 10. Do you know where WWJ is?"

"Yes, sir, I'll be there. Thank you."

At 10 a.m., sharp, I knocked on his door and the great man's voice said . . . "COME!"

The thin, pale, aging radio pioneer tilted back in his chair and got right down to business.

"So you think you want a career in radio, young man?"

"I don't know that much about it. I know I love sports; I loved being around the stadium like that and watching Mr. Heilmann do his games."

"Well, that's not radio. Radio is writing, selling, creative ideas, directing and producing. But mostly selling. Announcers just sit here and keep the sound going."

"Could I do that?"

"Do what?"

"What you just said."

"What appealed to you the most?"

I thought long about my answer, then decided to be just plain honest. "All of it. Whatever it would take to be in radio."

"Are you prepared to go to a four-year university and study hard?"

"Well, I don't have the money and my high school grades weren't that red-hot, but if that's what it takes, then I'll do it somehow."

"There are two schools I would recommend. Wayne University right here and Michigan State. State is the best."

"That's where I'd like to go to school. I've been on that campus a couple of times. And they have a radio school?"

"That's what I just said. They have their own radio station, too, WKAR, a 5,000 watter. Good school."

"What should I do next, Mr. Tyson?"

"First write for an application. With the war going on they'd

13

probably welcome you with open arms. Their enrollment is down about 50%. Fill it out and see if they'll accept you. They'll check with your high school and let you know."

He wished me well and I headed back to Birmingham inspired to do something positive for the first time in years. My head was swimming.

The next day my "Angel" at the office told me to whom I should write and what to say. Five days later the application was at the house and back in the mail the next day. Now it was nervous time. Naturally at that young age, a ripe old 18, all kinds of reasons popped up as to why I would be turned down. Grades were number one, not really believing that I belonged at a university was number two, and where would all this education get me was number three.

Down deep I wanted a better life. Whether I knew it or not, I was subconsciously praying for the bigger and better life. And suddenly, like magic, the right ideas, the right people, the right timing all came together at the right moment.

Michigan State accepted me. A letter to that effect arrived from the dean of students, Tom King. He invited me to the campus to talk about my major and housing. I got a day off and caught a bus for East Lansing. The campus was the prettiest, most sensational thing I had seen. I got goose bumps all over. Mr. King was waiting for me.

After discussing my major, he changed the subject. "Housing will be something you'll want to get at right away. Dorms are open only to women now because of the shortage we have. When some of the returning veterans come back they will get first choice when new dorms are built. So you will be living off campus in private housing. Here is a list of available rooms. You might try Mrs. Armstrong. She's on Kedzie. That's two blocks from the east end of the campus. Most of your classes will be in the Auditorium Building, which is also on the east end of the campus."

I wrapped things up and headed for 237 Kedzie and Mrs. Armstrong. She wasn't too encouraging.

"Really, I don't have anything right now . . . ," and she paused looking right through me to somewhere.

"I can't be kept out of my right place," whirred through my mind. "OK then," I began, showing my disappointment. "Mr. King felt this would be a good place for me. But thank you anyway." And I started down the steps.

"You know, I do have a smaller room that I could turn into a bedroom. Would you like to see it?"

"Sure, you never know," I said, turning quickly, thinking how dumb that sounded.

14

Up the stairs we both went to the second floor. I could see three good-sized bedrooms each with twin beds and two desks in them. I was beginning to get excited. Then she opened a door into what looked like a large closet but with a window looking westward toward the campus. It smelled musty and unused. I sagged noticeably. She rushed to open the window, which, amazingly, opened. The sales pitch began in earnest.

"You would have a nice view of the campus." I could see the tops of trees, the tower of Beaumont Tower and a smokestack with MSC painted on it. Whooppee!

"I could put a bed in here, a nice chest of drawers here," indicating a spot now occupied by boxes, "and a desk right here. Would that be satisfactory, Richard?"

I quickly weighed my options. A private room would cost more, which I didn't think would fit my meager budget, but the privacy angle really appealed to me. I guess I looked a bit disappointed or doubtful or something. She must have felt she was losing me rapidly.

"Of course, I couldn't charge you what I charge for the other rooms, this being smaller and all. This room would be half of that."

"That would work out fine," I said quickly, but not too quickly. All I could think of was being in my "right place". . . closet or no closet. We reviewed what was to be done and away I went.

The time flashed by, thank heaven. General Motors Truck Division, Material Control Department, said goodbye quietly with a couple of handshakes, a few good lucks and maybe one "come back and see us."

With my limited wardrobe, enough money in the bank to last me maybe two years, if I watched every penny, I was driven by my parents to East Lansing and my newly furnished closet on Kedzie Avenue on a bright Sunday afternoon.

Mrs. Armstrong had done a nice job fixing up my room, trying desperately to impress upon my parents how homey it would be. They weren't buying it. Of course they weren't renting it either. I was. And the price was right.

Thanks to Dean of Students Tom King I was invited to try out for the cheerleading squad. I had included Cheerleading on my application. Not many people were trying out; in fact I was the only freshman, so I wasn't too sure of my odds. But I was determined to give it a 110% effort.

Bob Turner, a senior, was the captain and showed us a few of the basic moves, and he and Rollie Young demonstrated a couple of cheers.

When it was my turn, I decided to let it all hang out. I over-

15

extended every motion, yelling at the top of my lungs.

"Great job, Dick," said Bob, smiling broadly. "Tell you what. We're having a pep rally for the Michigan game in the Union, 7 p.m. next Monday, the first day of classes. You be there and we'll give you a shot at a real crowd. OK?"

"Yes, sir, I'll be there."

The evening arrived and when Turner spotted me, he waved me up to the front of the lobby where they were holding the rally. The crowd was small. A few of the players were there. Coach Charlie Bachman was there. Turner and Young gave a cheer, then Bachman spoke and during his remarks Turner asked me if I wanted to try one.

"Yeah . . . I really would. What do you want me to do?"

"Why not a Green and White, Fight, Fight. They all know that one. I'll introduce you."

Bachman mumbled on a bit more, saying very little. But of course, you know why I say that.

Turner did the honors. I grabbed the megaphone, which was almost my size and which the crowd thought was hilarious, announced my yell, and I found myself back at my old stomping grounds. Boy, it felt good. I was a bit sloppy but no one noticed. They yelled. Bob motioned for me to do another one, and the crowd got more and more excited. And so did I. And so did Turner and Young. I got the feeling, glancing at them during the cheers, that I had a chance at the squad. I gave them a big finish, jumped as high as I could, which was about 2½ inches, and ran back to the rest of the squad, leaping and cavorting about. The crowd kept yelling and applauding, and the other cheerleaders were patting me on the back. I gave the crowd one more "fight" move, raising my fist sharply into the air, and they responded in one loud "FIGHT!" What a moment!

Turner wrapped it up. The students left slowly with some of them coming up to me saying all kinds of nice things. All Bob would say was, "OK, everyone, see you at practice next week." I asked Rollie on the way out to my bike who was going to Ann Arbor for the game.

"Jim doesn't know yet, but probably just the regulars." And with that he hurried off.

I didn't get to go. Bob said I wasn't ready yet. Neither was the team. They lost 40-0.

That first week provided one of the big turning points in my whole life. I've said before that if you know you are in your right place and going in the right direction, and you maintain a positive attitude, the right people will be there when you most need them. Dr. Robert Coleman, station manager of WKAR, was a prime example.

After my nine o'clock History class, and with an hour to spare, I took the long trek up four flights of stairs in the lobby of the Auditorium Building to take a look at our Michigan State radio station—WKAR. Ty Tyson had recommended it highly and if I was going to be a first-class sports announcer like him someday, I felt it was time for me to inform the manager.

At the top of the stairs was a small entryway, almost a lobby, and in a small office was the manager. The small plate beside the door read: Dr. Robert Coleman, Station Manager. The door was open; he was in his office, so I knocked on the door frame.

"Yes, young man," he said, looking me up and down quickly, "what can I do for you?"

"Dr. Coleman, my name is Dick Beals. I'm a freshman, and I'd like to sign up for a sports announcing job here. Ty Tyson at WWJ suggested that I see you about it." A little exaggeration but I wanted to make a big impression.

"You know Ty Tyson, do you?"

"Oh sure, he recommended I come to State and major in radio broadcasting."

"And you're a sports announcer, are you?" he asked kindly, knowing darn well I wasn't.

"Well, I haven't had much experience but that's what I want to do in radio . . . that, plus regular announcing."

"Well," he said, and he opened the big drawer in his desk looking for something, "let's get an application out of here for you. It's not every day that a sports announcer comes in here looking for a job. Yes . . . here it is." He opened a file folder and took out a two-page form.

"Take this home with you, fill it out and get it back to me," he said, handing it to me. Then, as I was looking it over quickly, he settled back in his chair, folded his arms across his chest, closed his eyes as if looking for inspiration, took off his glasses and looking at me kind of funny, he began slowly with the softest, kindest voice I had ever heard.

"Son, you know, announcers are a dime a dozen. Everyone wants to be an announcer. Have you ever considered acting on radio?"

"Acting?"

"Acting. Doing dramatic parts on radio shows."

"No, not really."

"Have you ever done any acting?"

"Sure. Motion pictures for Jam Handy, Wilding and Ross Roy. Kids' parts. And school plays, variety shows and things. I like to sing."

"You know . . . we have a new radio show coming up this

fall called Rural School Music Time. It will be the music curriculum for the schools throughout the state that have no music teacher. There's a part of a boy about 10. I think you ought to audition for that part. You might like it.''

I guess I paused a bit too long. He came in with the kill.

"You'd probably get to sing, too.''

"Could I still be a sports announcer?''

"If something came up, sure. Of course Larry Frymire does all our sports announcing now but you never know. I'll have your application right here just in case . . . .''

"When is the audition?''

"Friday, 4 p.m., right here in studio A. Do you have a class then?''

"No, and we won't have cheerleader practice either because of the home game with Kentucky. I can make it.''

"Excellent. I'll tell J. Kenneth Richards, the director, that you'll be here.''

Dr. Robert J. Coleman could have just as easily thrown me down the four flights of stairs when I walked into his office. But he didn't. Here was this brash kid announcing that WKAR's new sports announcer had just arrived. "Ty Tyson sent me'' indeed! He knew Ty Tyson and he knew that Tyson knew that I wasn't any kind of sports announcer yet invented. He knew, just listening to my childlike voice, that I could never be taken seriously as an announcer, staff or sports or any kind. He knew exactly where I belonged.

And, bless him, he had the presence of mind, the composure, the experience, the patience and the thoughtfulness to redirect me. Another Angel Voice heard from.

It was to be the single most important piece of advice I ever received in my entire life. Thank you, Dr. Robert J. Coleman, wherever you are!

The audition? It wasn't, really. There weren't that many college kids with a childlike voice with acting experience. But they made it look and sound like an audition with the usual, "we'll let you know'' line. Gullible me, I believed J. Kenneth Richards to the hilt. I sweated it out over the weekend. But early the next week one of my speech professors, Dr. Don Buell, told me that J. Kenneth Richards wanted to see me at WKAR at four that afternoon. I was there—early.

"OK, Dick, you're Johnny,'' began the smallish, young, dark-haired director, going a mile a minute. "Elaine Jason will be Mary, Bob Kamen is the announcer and Bob Huber will be Kiseemee. Get me your class schedule so we can work out a time for rehearsal and recording for all of you. The Music Department will also be involved, and some of their musicians

18

and singers will do the show."

Rural School Music Time was a half-hour show. Kiseemee, the Magician of All the Ages, told Johnny and Mary a story about a composer or an opera or related some musical education of some sort. If a song was needed the "Choir," accompanied by a magical string quartet, just happened to be there and sang when called upon.

As unprofessional as we were, our director was tough and demanding. Some of the points he made in the fall of 1945 still echo in my ears today. Diction was number one.

"Johnny, sound that 'i-n-g'," he would say. "By the time some kid in a noisy classroom in the upper peninsula on a small radio hears this being played off an electrical transcription here, he'll have to strain to hear it. And he shouldn't have to. I want to hear every vowel and every consonant."

That sound advice got me more jobs later than anything I ever learned. That and staying with the script, and picking up missed cues, and inserting a line to keep the show going without missing a beat.

We were doing a Stephen Foster episode, and it came time to have our instantly appearing singers slide in with "Swing Low, Sweet Chariot." But they forgot how to "appear" or something. So did the string quartet. Kiseemee said, "Yes children, Stephen Foster wrote this song, familiar to us all . . . ".

No singers among them. I glanced over and they just weren't with it. So I started singing the song—no music, no lead sheet, no key. I knew it by heart from years back and just let it all hang out.

At the end of my rendition, Kiseemee, a music major, picked it right up with some ad lib that justified my action, and on we went with the show.

I was thrilled to pieces. If this was radio acting, I loved it. J. Kenneth Richard's reaction? "Good pickup, Johnny."

Winning a job on the cheerleading squad was important too. The second Saturday was our first home game, with Kentucky, and I was hoping against hope to make the squad. In my favor were experience and the novelty of my size. Against me was my total lack of acrobatic skills. I couldn't jump over my own shadow. When I tried a forward roll, jumping over another cheerleader, I landed on the very top of my head and crunch went my neck. Enough of that nonsense. Every night that week, though, I grabbed one of the guys and dragged him kicking and screaming down the stairs to our front yard and had him watch me go through all the routines.

"Pick me apart, Russell; what am I doing wrong?" I panted.

"I don't know anything about cheerleading. Milking cows,

yeah. But I don't know what to look for."

"OK, I'll do the locomotive once more. Are my moves sharp enough? Am I leading you or following you? Try to remember that you're forty rows up, which is like being down there by that last car."

At that Russ headed down the street.

"Where are you going? I need you right here," I shouted, to no avail.

"I'm going to sit on that car down there," he said, talking over this shoulder. And he did. "OK, what's the yell?" he shouted after climbing onto the roof of the car.

It was quite a scene. Here's this kid with the high, squeaky voice announcing—no, screaming at the top of his lungs—something about a Green and White, Fight, Fight, giving the count, jumping up and down. And there, halfway down the street, sitting on top of some poor neighbor's car roof is some big guy following the squeaky kid's motions and yelling back at the top of his lungs.

Now comes the critique. What we really needed were two tin cans and string, but no such luck.

"Your moves are too tight. Too close to your body. Let your arms fly farther away from you. I can hardly see any movement at all."

So I tried it again. Now porch lights were beginning to come on. Curtains were parting here and there. Folks were slowly but surely coming out onto front porches.

Undaunted we go through all the routines. Finally Russell jumps off the car after my fifth Green and White, clapping his hands and pumping his fist into the air and shouting . . . "Yeah, yeah, yeah, that's it."

Assorted neighbors also applaud, either from gratitude that we'll be quitting soon or from appreciation of my efforts or both.

"Really, Russ . . . could you see improvement? Is it getting there?"

"Yeah, no kidding, it's a lot better. Even from the 'top row' out there I could follow you."

"Let's hope they let a freshman make the squad. The odds are against it, but it won't be because I didn't give it 110%."

The next night the same thing except for one difference. The neighbor must have seen us coming because he moved his car into his driveway. No problem for Russ. He could also climb trees in addition to milking cows. If the scene was hilarious the night before, having Russ up in that tree yelling his lungs out was some kind of picture to remember.

Head Cheerleader Bob Turner waited until after Thursday's

20

practice to make the announcement. Practice that afternoon took place for some reason in the 22,000-seat stadium. It was a dark, cold, misty, cold-front-approaching type of late afternoon. I was looking at him all during practice for some kind of indication about my chances but could see nothing. I knocked myself out trying to follow Russell's instructions. In fact, for every routine, I worked to an imaginary fan in the top row by the press box.

Turner said quietly, "OK, that's it. Let's head back for Jenison. Someone grab the megaphones." And we all grabbed jackets and things and headed back to the field house and a warm locker room.

Before I could get too far I felt a firm grip on my shoulder from behind. It was Turner.

"Do you think you could get some white pants and a green sweater by Saturday?" he asked, smiling.

"Really? Do you mean it, Bob? Did I make it?" I was darned near crying.

"Yeah, you really worked hard. You're good. The crowd's going to like you and probably make some noise for you. We'll see Saturday."

"I'll sure try."

"How about the pants and sweater? Can you get them? We just don't have anything here that will fit you. We've been checking all week."

"All week?" I thought. He's known it all week. Poor Russ. "I'll call home tonight. The sweater I can handle, I think. But the white pants . . . I don't know if they make them my size. And I can't afford to have them tailor made. But I'll know tomorrow."

"OK, head on back. I have to give some bad news to a few folks here and I'm not very good at it." With that, he patted me on the top of my bruised and knotted head and ran back to the others.

It's a long way from the stadium back to Jenison Field House. But not on that cold, rainy, dark, late afternoon. I floated. My head was swimming. In one week I had started college, won a lead role on a radio show and now had made the cheerleading squad. THINK BIG!

21

"Adventures in Music", a weekly radio show, before a "live" audience, and beamed to children in schools all over the state of Michigan. With Dick, is Marian Cannon, the "Sweetheart of Sigma Chi", and Bob Huber, as Kiseemee.

Fall of 1945. Dick at age 18, a freshman at Michigan State College, is practicing a "Yea State" as a Varsity Cheerleader for the Spartans. At the left, Doris Guth and on the right, Yvonne Means.

The 1946 Michigan State Varsity Cheerleading squad, prior to the Spartan's basketball season. Captain Rollie Young, in white sweater, to Dick's right.

Fall, 1945. Michigan State Varsity Cheerleaders. Dick, somehow, found some white pants, but had to settle for a blue-green sweater. With World War II winding down, women outnumbered men on campus, 3 to 1, as evidenced by the cheerleading unit.

On a bitter cold, windy, Michigan day, January 1947, the all-male Michigan State cheerleading squad, poses on the steps of Jenison Fieldhouse. Note Dick's numeral sweater, signifying his first varsity letter.

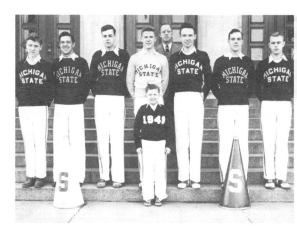

3

A Summer Job Saves the Day

As the end of my freshman year approached, three major problems faced me. Housing, job and money.

Mrs. Armstrong announced that her nephew would be coming home from the service, getting married and needing the upstairs living quarters. Back to Tom King I hustled and he gave me a list of recommended rooms.

As usual, positive thinking prevailed once again. An Angel must have been looking out for me because I found a room, suddenly vacated, just across the street from the middle of the campus. Again it was a double room but they agreed to let me have it all to myself and charge me only half price. I leveled with them. I told them this was probably my last year because my funds would barely last three more terms.

Number two problem was a job. There weren't any. Returning veterans got their jobs back, and college students didn't have a chance. I applied for unemployment compensation but that was denied. That summer I lived at home and did work around the house to help out. But zero income.

So that was my situation. However, a family summer vacation turned out to be one of the biggest breaks yet for me and proved once again that "where there's a will there's a way."

The Angel Voices were at it again.

While at Traverse City, we took a side trip to Mackinac Island. I didn't want to go, but dad insisted, so off we went. We took the ferry boat across and who but two fellow State freshmen were working on the boat. More Spartans I knew were working on the dock. Up at the Grand Hotel were a bunch of bellhops, some of whom were friends from school. I took one look at the swimming pool, the golf course and that hotel and thought . . . this is fore me! It never occurred to me to talk to the manager or someone about a job for the next summer. During the long drive back to our cottage, I silently kicked myself.

Then I said to no one in particular, "I wish I had talked to the manager or someone. That was dumb."

More silence. Then a new voice shattered the quiet. It was my dad.

"He wasn't in. Neither of the owners was there."

I almost fainted from shock. Then I asked the dumbest question of the day. "How did you find that out?"

"I asked."

With that, he pulled a small slip of paper out of his pocket and handed it over his shoulder to me.

"Offices are in Chicago at that address. Names are Woodfill. Jim is the vice president and manager. His dad's president. They'll be back in Chicago October 1."

That's all. End of lecture. But for my quiet, reserved dad that was a ton. He wasn't telling me to write them. He wouldn't offer to help me write the letter. He would never mention the subject again . . . ever. That was it. It was up to me to do it. But for him to get that information was miraculous. He might have hinted about it, looked around for a brochure, asked my mother if she thought it was a good idea, which meant that she was to do it . . . but not my dad. He did it.

In no time I was back on campus, a full-fledged sophomore. I mailed Mr. Woodfill's letter so that it would be on his desk by October 1. The Book Cadillac Hotel experience was mentioned with references listed on a separate page. Bob Baker, one of the bellhops, said to list extracurricular activities at State. So I put down cheerleading, Student Council and Adventures in Music and stuff like that. I applied for a page boy's job.

Within a week I received a response at my new residence. It was from Jim Woodfill. His opening sentence shot me down. "We don't employ page boys at the Grand Hotel."

I let the letter hit my lap and just sat and stared at the wall. Suddenly, all I could think of was my shrinking bank balance. How can you be positive when your one big chance says no? I regrouped and, not interested in all his good reasons, finished reading the letter.

However, we do have another position we'd like you to consider. It is called Lobby Server. You would serve tea and cookies in the afternoons from four to six and demitasse in the evenings from 7 to 11. Your pay would be $50 per month, room and board included. The Lobby Server also serves alcoholic beverages. The position usually receives ample tips if performed properly.

"Your hours would be 4 p.m. to 12 a.m. daily, seven days a week. You would report for work when the hotel opens June 15th. The hotel closes September 10. If you are interested let me know as soon as possible. We have several applicants for the job."

Sincerely yours,
James Woodfill

A job offer. An honest-to-goodness job offer. A possibility of another term if I could make the tips. I got my reply out that afternoon.

That evening I had a chance to think things out. If this was right, then the needed supply would be there and school was the right place. "I am always in my right place. No one or no thing or no event can keep me out of my right place." I tried to know that the supply would be there, whether it was the Grand Hotel or what. "But keep a positive thought and go about your business." With that prayer in mind I fell asleep.

A week later I found another letter with the Grand Hotel logo waiting for me on the steps leading upstairs, our special reserved spot. I grabbed it and raced upstairs.

Dear Mr. Beals;

You have been selected to be the Lobby Server at the Grand Hotel for the coming 1947 season.

He repeated the dates the hotel would be open, when I should report and other details.

I closed my tear-filled eyes, said a little prayer and just sat there for a while. It had demonstrated to me once again how things work out if you let them. How you must stay out of the way with negative thinking and know if it is right, it will be. If it isn't right, then look ahead to the next opportunity because it will surely be there. But don't look back at the seeming failure begrudging your luck, or fate, or politics or the favorite line of the loser, "It isn't what you know but who you know." It's YOU you have to know. Not someone else. Only YOU can help you.

Thinking back to the summer vacation at Traverse City and the side trip my dad planned, "just for something to do," caused me to consider another point. If something is right, it will be right for everyone, not just me. It will solve a personnel problem for the hotel, provide better service and therefore enjoyment for the guests, take the pressure off my parents and, who knows, the continuing educational opportunities might be moving me onward and upwards to something important in life. It was an important moment for me and I was so grateful for the opportunity to move ahead one more giant step.

4
Good News and Bad News

As spring term flew by, my thoughts turned to the Grand Hotel and a chance at some income. My bank account was predictably at the "add a quart" line. The landlords did announce that the front room, which was a lot brighter than mine, would be available, if I wanted it. I agreed to take the larger, brighter room at the same reduced rate, pending sufficient funds to continue school.

The big day, or rather night, arrived when the train was to take me to Mackinaw City. With my meager wardrobe and golf clubs, my parents took me to the train in Detroit and my first experience with a lower berth.

The beautiful, sunny, warm Mackinac Island I remembered from August, was now cold and rainy. The magnificent Grand Hotel seemed to shiver in the dreariness. The ferry boat ride over was choppy and wet. The ride up the hill in the carriage to the Grand was choppier and wetter and smellier.

I found Mr. Woodfill, who greeted me and had a fellow Michigan State bellhop show me to the Pool House and my room. The Grand stood high on a hill and everything else was below it. Especially the Pool House. It was an old, damp, cold, uninspired, wornout wood frame structure and was to be home for three months. It was free and now I knew why.

Later, I found my way to the tailor shop. They didn't have a uniform that came close to fitting me.

"Here's what we have, little man," said the woman in charge.

As I grabbed the pants, I also grabbed her wrist, firmly. "Ma'am," I began quietly, "Call me Beals, or Dick, or sir, but never 'little man.'"

She let go the pants and turned back to her sewing machine.

"Try the pants on and let's go from there," she mumbled.

She had a long way to go, both in the pants and in her manners. The pants had to be taken in everywhere. It would be a major operation. The short white jacket was closer. It would require only minor surgery. I would be wearing my own white shirts, which they would launder for me and the black bow tie was designed to fit anybody. So I was set. But it would take at least three days for the first fitting.

I found the superintendent of bellmen and the bell captains, all pros, and the assistant manager who explained my duties.

I followed him out to the kitchen and with the help of the head kitchen steward we located the brass samovar that was used to serve tea. It had a kind of smokestack, down which I was to drop a can of Sterno, followed by a lighted match. The idea was to hit the can of Sterno with the lighted match, ignite the Sterno and thence keep the tea hot. That was what was supposed to happen. I found several ways to make things go wrong. One, the lighted match would miss the open 2½-inch-wide can or, two, the match would hit it but the match would have gone out. So you ask, "why not light the can first then drop it in. The answer is that if it doesn't get seated just right in its little pocket, it tilts and the ignited Sterno runs all over the place. I solved the problem in my usual way. I got someone else to do it.

At night I served demitasse from a silver coffee server into demitasse cups. It was difficult to keep the coffee hot, so I had to make many trips back to the kitchen to replenish the supply. But my advisor back on campus was right . . . mostly I served drinks. The tea and demitasse service was just for show. Cookies went with the tea, but they were consumed mostly by the bellmen who devised ingenious ways to snitch them, causing me no end of problems, which pleased them even more. However, there were tons in the kitchen so I just kept the trays filled.

But that's getting ahead of the clock and the calendar. It took five days for the grim-faced seamstress to prepare a uniform for me, just in time for the opening. The first group in was the National Auto Dealers Association. At that point in history, car dealers were making big profits. Some of them—no, most of them, decided to spend a lot of it at the Grand. They were big tippers. It got us off to a great start.

And then, quite by accident I got a big break. The Angels were looking out for me. I was serving drinks in the lobby on Saturday afternoon, with one ear listening to the recorded music playing over the PA system. It was a song I knew, "Smoke Gets in Your Eyes," and very softly I sang along. The social director overheard me and as I went by her desk back to my service table, she got up and followed me.

Seeing her approach, I stopped singing, but she said, "Oh, please continue, that's my favorite song."

So I picked up the melody again and continued softly, singing just to her.

"Oh, that's so nice," she said when I finished. "Where did you learn to sing like that?"

"I'm not a singer, really, compared to our music majors. I just sing."

"What else do you sing?"

"Anything if you have the words."

"How about the old favorites?"

"You mean like 'Shine on Harvest Moon,' 'For Me and My Gal,' 'Daisy,' 'Irish Eyes,' 'Wild Irish Rose.' I know all of those."

She thought long and hard. "You know, I'm going to ask Mr. Woodfill if you couldn't help me with something. Tomorrow, Sunday night around 7, he wants me to have a community sing right here in the lobby. We'll have a few members of our orchestra here and I'm to lead the singing. And I can't sing a lick. I'm going to ask him if you couldn't do it for me. Would you be willing?"

"Is the Pope Catholic, lady," I thought. But I said, "Oh sure, I'd love to."

Permission was granted. I guess he also knew she couldn't sing.

Sunday arrived and the orchestra leader and I went over the songs, found stacks of song sheets that we could hand out, and got the sound system set up with a two-foot riser for me.

By now it had grown into a big production because the NADA convention manager had gotten involved, publicized it, and made it the official closing program for the convention. He came up to me all excited just as we were about to get started.

"Now listen, Dick, we need a big finish. It's Sunday. How about doing something dramatic."

"You mean like a hymn?"

"Yeah, but I doubt if anyone here knows one."

"I meant that I would sing the hymn, solo. The Lord's Prayer would be fitting."

"Yeah, but we don't have music for that," chimed in the orchestra leader.

"That's OK, just give me the key of C and let me do it in the clear. If you want to do some soft harmony, go ahead."

The convention manager was ecstatic. And so was I. I hadn't come there to light cans of Sterno.

At 6:45, people started filtering in from the dining room, and soon the huge lobby was standing room only. It was going to be a tough place to work. The lobby was easily 300 feet long and 35 feet narrow. I was positioned in the middle, to work both ends. But I was rarin' to go. At shortly after 7:00 the social director introduced me. We moved right into the first song and the audience was soon singing at the top of their lungs.

The crowd grew and grew. They were now outside on the porch singing, sitting atop the registration desk, on the floor, just jammed in everywhere . . . and they were all mine.

Thirty minutes later, when we had exhausted our song sheets, singing some twice, the convention manager jumped up onto the riser and grabbed the mike from me. I really didn't want

27

to give it to him. "Hey folks . . . isn't Dick great!" he shouted. Thunderous applause and cheering followed. "Listen now. Quiet." And he waited until they were. "Dick is going to close this greatest of all meetings by singing the Lord's Prayer." He was interrupted with ohs and ahs from the 500-plus there. "Now listen. Dick is working his way through Michigan State. Let's help him a little bit. We're going to pass the hat while he's singing our closing song and you help him out, OK? How about it?"

I didn't hear anyone vote no.

I waited for quiet. Paused. Paused for absolute silence and then nodded at the piano player. While the chord was played I said softly, "We've surely enjoyed having you with us these past few days. Please have a safe trip home and take this prayer with you."

Talk about a special happening! The orchestra harmonized softly just at the right moments. The sound system carried my warmed-up voice to every corner of the hotel and there wasn't a sound except for the Lord's Prayer. Eyes glistened, tears were wiped, heads bowed, and in the background I could catch glimpses of the convention manager prodding the college bellhops to get the cardboard boxes distributed. I made a special effort to control my breathing for the last big finish of *A-men*. I did and the applause was deafening, with folks jumping onto their feet. I waved good-bye, jumped off the riser, and headed for the bell captain's desk. It took me 30 minutes to go 45 feet. I was mobbed.

When sanity prevailed and I could get off by myself, there was Jimmy Woodfill. "Nice job. Plan on doing it every Sunday." He turned on his heel and departed.

My roommates and the convention manager finally got all the boxes gathered up, and when we got off by ourselves we started counting it. There was no change, just paper money. It totaled $125. I couldn't believe it. What a way to start a week. I took it to the cashier and got it changed into 20's, tucked it away and sought out the convention manager.

"I can't thank you enough. This will really help the cause."

"It was a real touch, Dick. Everyone is really pleased. You can really handle yourself in front of a microphone."

"Right now I'm an amateur but that's why I'm at State, to learn how."

"See you next year?" he asked.

"I'll sure apply but it's up to the management."

We shook hands and I went back to work. My pals in the cocktail lounge had taken over for me during the counting but when I returned they showed me who was having what and

28

I took over.

The guests were most complimentary and the tips were enormous. Time flew by—thank goodness, because I was running out of gas. By 10 o'clock the place started thinning out and by 11 p.m., when it was quiet, my roommates and I called it a day and headed down the long stairs to the Pool House.

I wanted to split some of the money with them but they assured me that the head guy had taken care of them. I tucked the money into my hiding place in my drawer, and was the first to fall asleep. What a day. What a start.

The next morning I slowly came to and decided to get up and get breakfast. I rummaged around in my drawer for some clean socks and decided to count my money just once more. It was gone. I pulled the contents of that drawer apart piece by piece but no cash. I sat down on my bed in complete shock and a few tears. Why? Who? It couldn't have been one of my college friends. That left one of the pros. But which one? About then Gene Marcus, a roommate from Holland, Michigan, came in from his shower. He took one look at me and knew something was wrong. "What's the matter, Dick? Don't feel well?"

"Money's all gone. Someone stole it. Everything." I was almost in tears. I could hardly talk.

He sat down on his lower bunk, not having the slightest idea of what to say. "Is there anything I can do?"

I just shook my head and stared straight ahead. Some of the other folks wandered in and Gene told them the news. They tried to comfort me but they couldn't. I left to wash up and after a short while came back to get dressed. Gene had been elected chairman.

"We'll find out who did it. In the meantime if you need any money just ask." I nodded to all of them, got dressed in silence and for once appreciated the long walk up the hill to breakfast.

The word spread like proverbial wildfire. Sympathy poured in from all the guys.

Work went on. That night, though, a strange thing happened. One of the pros went berserk. He got drunk and was throwing things all over the Pool House. In the dark he came into our room, picked up a heavy glass ash tray and hurled it blindly. It missed Gene's head by an inch and put a huge dent in the metal bed frame.

He was screaming all kinds of things about his wife and that she was cheating on him and he would get her. In the morning he was gone. We all, to the man, felt that my money was on its way to Florida. Quite by accident we proved it almost immediately.

It was Dick's pleasure to close each
Sunday's community sing with the Lord's
Prayer. At his first performance the
proberbial "hat" was passed and earned
Dick $125. Unfortunately a fellow bellman
ran off to Florida with it.

The new bellman staff, on the
porch of the Grand Hotel,
Mackinac Island, June 1947.
The Grand still employs mostly
college students from around
the USA.

The new Lobby Server at the Grand, with his afternoon tea service. Note the dreaded Samovar. The seamstress wasn't truly inspired in custom tailoring his uniform either.

The Lobby Server working the 880 foot-long Grand Hotel porch.

5

The Ups and Downs of Growing Up

The robbery meant starting over financially but it taught me a valuable lesson, one that I had not learned being brought up in a small town. People steal. I had never encountered anything like that. It had never occurred to me it could happen. But of course I had never had one hundred dollars either.

The bozo who left town was good riddance as far as the college crew was concerned. He was vulgar, violent and abusive. Because he left with some hotel property, the two local police officers were called in by the management. Gene told them about my loss too.

"Do you have any evidence, Dick?" asked the polite captain.

"No, not really, but he bunked with us. He could easily have known where I kept the money. I made no secret of it."

"Well, without any hard evidence, there's not much we can do—you know that."

"We'll prove it," said Gene. "He wasn't that bright and he was stoned, so he just might have been careless."

"Keep us posted then. I can't promise even with proof that we can get your money back but I'd love to nail him. He caused us problems all over the island." With that the captain and his lieutenant drove away in the only car allowed on the island. And we all went back to work.

The bozo *was* careless. There was a small restaurant and bar just south of the hotel called Mary's Pantry. Some of us dropped in there once in a while when we were walking back up the hill from downtown. Gene, Bobby, Moose and I were sitting there nursing Cokes when Gene decided to cash in a bunch of his tips. They totaled about $25, so he asked the waitress if he could have a $20 bill and a $5.

"Geez, kid, we just opened and I don't think the boss is back from the bank yet with our big bills," she said, chomping on her gum, "but let me check."

Back she came shaking her head no. "No dice. Nuthin'. Can you wait a bit? He'll be back in about 20 minutes. Or I can get you fives."

"No, I don't want fives, and I can't wait," said Gene politely.

"Well, wait a minute, maybe I got a twenty in my purse. Hold on." And off she wiggled through the door to the kitchen, cleverly marked IN. Twenty seconds later out she popped from the other door holding up a 20-dollar bill for us to see. "I did have it. Kept it out from my tips the other night. First time anyone tipped me $20. Hate to part with it but why not."

She laid the twenty down in the middle of the table as Gene reached in his hip pocket for his wallet.

I just sat there staring at the twenty. I had seen it before.

"What's the matter, Dick? See something?" asked Gene.

I picked it up to have a closer look. It had a red smear across the face like from lipstick or a crayon. It was well worn.

"This was one of my $20s that I got from the front desk Sunday night," I said, looking from face to face.

"Sure?" said Gene.

"Sure!"

"Let's have a little talk with our waitress," suggested Moose.

Gene signaled her and over she ambled, order pad poised. Gene took over.

"Where'd you say you got this twenty, Miss?"

"Why?" she asked, taking a step back.

"Just wondering. I'm studying criminology at school and this bill is defaced and I'd like to know why you marked it up like this." He even almost convinced me with his criminology line—except he was attending Hope College and was a seminary student.

"Well, geez, I didn't do it. It was a tip. I don't examine bills when I take them. I just take 'em and run."

"When did you get this tip, Miss?" asked Moose politely.

"Geez, let's see. Today's uh, uh . . . "

"Thursday," prompted Moose.

"Yeah, today is Thursday. Yeah, Thursday. Sure. Uh—must have been Monday night. Late. Real late. Just about closing time."

Gene took over the grilling. I was really impressed.

"When do you close up here?"

"Two a.m."

"So it was actually Tuesday morning, early?"

"Geez, yeah . . . but who cares?"

"We do," said Moose quickly and seriously.

"Do you remember who gave you the tip?" asked Gene about as disinterested as he could sound.

"Sure, one of the bellhops from the Grand. Real jerk. Mean, too. Smashed when he came in, screamin' and yellin'. The boss had to threaten him three times. He finally booted him out."

"But during the evening he tipped you with this twenty," stated Gene quietly. "He must have liked you."

"Sure, he knew class when he saw it," she said, fussing with her hair a bit and smoothing out her apron. "Poor guy, found out his wife's been cheatin' on him. Took it real hard. Said he was headin' back to Florida to settle her hash, once and for all."

31

We all looked at each other, trying to show no emotion, but wanting to. It was a "good news-bad news" situation. But I was surely proud of Moose and Gene for the way they handled the "investigation."

"Well, we thank you for all your help. Thanks for the twenty," smiled Gene. When she was out of earshot Gene posed the next question.

"Well, what do we do now?"

"Hang on to the twenty, Gene," suggested Moose. "Dick, you talk to the captain and tell him about this conversation and let him take it from there. How's that sound?"

We all agreed and headed back to the Pool House.

As we were walking through the woods, taking a shortcut, I remembered to tell them some important news.

"Woodfill came up to me last night and announced a plan for us to keep our money safe." Hearing no reaction, I continued. "He has set up extra safety deposit boxes for us and we can cash in every night if we want to. The person at the front desk gives us a special envelope to put the money in, we tear off the top part of the flap which has a number on it, seal the flap and the envelope goes in the safe."

"How do we know which envelope is ours?" asked Bobby, choking on his cigarette.

"Geez, kid," chomped Gene, imitating the waitress, "Ders a number on da envelope dat matches the number on da flap. Geez!"

That was all it took to break the tension of the past four days and we fell all over ourselves laughing the rest of the way. We just couldn't stop laughing. Poor Bobby thought we were laughing at him but we weren't. We giggled about that all summer. After that whenever Gene walked through the lobby and he knew we were looking, he would go into his "waitress wiggle" imitation and break us up. What a bunch.

The captain listened intently, examined the $20, exchanged it for one he had and still made no promises.

"We've traced him. He's broke. There is really not much we can do. With a little pressure we could get him to admit he stole your money, Dick, but it isn't enough to extradite him back here. It's a misdemeanor and so he's convicted. He still couldn't pay you back the $100. You agree?"

"I'd like him to admit he stole it."

"OK, I'll tell the Florida guys that. They're keeping their eyes on him. If he gets out of line they'll nail him. Use your situation as a wedge."

"Fine with me. It was an expensive lesson. Glad it wasn't more."

"OK, 'deputies,' thanks for your help. Good work. Proud of you. See you around campus, or something like that." He laughed at his little joke and left.

All in all we were pretty proud of our detective work. Another good thing came out of the incident. The superintendent and the two bell captains felt pretty bad about it, inasmuch as it was one of their "pro team." They went out of their way to treat us right the rest of the summer. In fact, they were downright polite.

The Sunday sing-alongs continued. Gene was involved in an embarrassing experience. Embarrassing for him but hilarious for the rest of us.

Mr. Woodfill suggested for one convention that the Lord's Prayer wouldn't be appropriate so he suggested we finish with the national anthem. There was a big American flag on a six-foot pole standing near the orchestra and he thought it would be a real touch of dramatics for the flag to wave during the anthem. He asked Gene to set up a big fan about four feet away and turn it on "precisely at the drum roll."

It was a big fan—a big, powerful fan. While I introduced the final number and asked everyone to stand, Gene moved quietly into position and the drum roll commenced.

We were all singing to our heart's content, the fan blowing the flag dramatically. I glanced at Mr. Woodfill, who nodded at me with great pride. I glanced back at Gene between notes and his eyes were like saucers. And then I saw what he saw. The tassles on the flag had started swinging violently back and forth, getting higher and higher. Before Gene could stop the fan the tassles worked their way into the fan blades and all hell broke loose. Noise? Pandemonium? Oh my! Before Gene could restore order, the flag was down and the tassles were all chewed up, with bits and pieces landing everywhere. The orchestra and I gave the anthem a big finish, but by then I think I was the only one singing except for the back row, who couldn't see what the trouble was all about.

Mr. Woodfill by now had disappeared back into his office. From that time on the social director and I planned the program.

The summer went by like lightning, and it was a real learning experience for the college crew. We instigated a baby-sitting and dog-sitting service, and organized hotel tours. The orchestra leader let me sing with his group once in a while, which was invaluable for me. We talked Mr. Woodfill into letting us put on a variety show, which I was nominated to emcee.

The last act at the Grand was to help close it down. The last guest had departed and we had to stay for two days to take inventory, take draperies down, turn in our uniforms and I forget all what.

I had called my parents and dad recommended I take my money out of the safety deposit box, get an escort to take me to the back, get a cashier's check and send it home Special Delivery. I wasn't sure about the escort part until our friend, the captain of the Island police department, found Moose, Gene and me working in the dining room counting flatware.

"I got good news and not so good news, young man." he said with his usual twinkle. "You were right about the man who stole your money. But we can't get it back. Thought you'd like to know."

"Did they get the jerk?" Gene asked.

"They got him. He went after his ex-wife and the Florida police got to him before he could do much damage. She filed charges, had witnesses, so he's in for a spell."

"How do you know he took Dick's money?" chimed in Moose.

"They asked him. Point blank. He said yes. Said he was sorry but he was broke, he needed it for boat and airfare and he took it. Nothing personal, he said. He knew where everyone kept their money and if it hadn't been yours, Dick, he would have gotten someone else's."

"Jerk!" Gene said, almost spitting.

"Did you guys have a good year other than that?"

All of us thought about the bank trip about the same time.

"Yes, we earned our pay." I opened cautiously. "By the way, Captain, could you do us a very special favor?"

"I guess so. What?"

"How about being here at 2:30 this afternoon and giving us a ride down to the bank?" said Gene, quickly.

"And then a ride to the post office," said Moose, jumping in.

The big captain thought a second, grinned and said, "For my special deputies . . . anything you say. See you at 2:30, men."

At 2:15 we picked up our stacks of little brown, numbered envelopes, got big manila envelopes from the secretary, and stuffed in our loot just in time to hear a short burst of the siren out in front. We played our ride downtown to the hilt. We were all very important and let everyone know it. At least I hope that's what they thought.

With our escort standing guard in the bank we all went to separate tellers and transacted our business. I hadn't kept track of my earnings so you can imagine how I felt when the teller said quietly, "That will be exactly $1,150."

"Eleven hundred and fifty dollars?" I exclaimed in shock. "Are you sure?"

"I'm sure," he answered a bit perturbed. "Who is the payee?"

34

"The who?"

"The payee. Who do you want the check made out to?"

I gave him my name, got the check, put it in the envelope I had prepared and off we went in the police car to the post office.

Our work completed, the good captain drove us slowly back up the hill to the magnificent edifice called the Grand. A storm was moving in, and not the usual warm summer rainstorm. You could see the cold, dreary, gray clouds out over Lake Michigan, west of the Straits of Mackinac. There was a fall chill in the air, and the island was strangely quiet for the first time since June.

The captain knew full well that the Grand had a lot of turnover but despite this knowledge he said he hoped we'd all be back next year, and have a good year in school and all that.

We thanked him and stood in a group as he made his way back down the long hill. When he was abeam the golf course we saw the red lights flash and heard his siren give a little squeal, and we all waved a final farewell.

The Grand did more than pad my bank account by $1,150. As my thoughts reviewed the scenes that were flashing in and out, I quietly shook my head in amazement at the opportunities that had allowed me to stumble, learn, grow, and mature, all packed into barely three months. The most valuable experience, career-wise, had been the singing with the orchestra and community singing on Sunday evenings. It had nothing to do with radio acting but it was performing, under pressure, in front of a critical audience. Next was learning about people. Psych courses at school are necessary but they don't help you get along with demanding guests, difficult managers and supervisors and annoying fellow workers. You're on your own and it is a tough, necessary experience – especially for someone slowly inching up to about 4'3" who can't fight back. Everyone knows it and, believe me, they take advantage of it.

So all in all, I accomplished the goal I set as the ferry boat had taken me and the family back to Mackinaw City 13 months before. I had my junior year paid for. And then some.

Maybe it was the cold or the mist but something was filling my eyes with tears. I was so grateful for the opportunity and I knew the source of all my good. I just closed my eyes for a spell and said a silent prayer of thanks.

6

A Glimpse of Things to Come

As the bus rolled up Grand River and the campus came into view, I couldn't get over how great it looked and how nice it was to be back. How I loved this place! It was worth all the working and scratching and summer jobs and General Motors. I belonged at Michigan State despite what my misguided high school teachers had me believe.

Because my new room wouldn't be ready for a couple of days, our radio director, J. Kenneth Richards, invited me to stay with them. They not only were ready for me, they even met my bus, which was a nice touch. In fact, because my bike was still in my landlord's locked garage, Mr. Richards went out of his way to drop me off here and there when it was necessary.

The only discouraging note was my first encounter with the new cheerleader coach, who was also the new gymnastics coach. Instead of telling me that he planned extensive tumbling routines, which we all knew I couldn't handle, he said all the wrong things and truly embarrassed me. "Beals, I want uniformity this year. So unless you can grow a foot and a half in three days, we can't use you." And then he laughed loud and long, until he realized that the other cheerleaders were just staring at him in disbelief. This made me so mad, I got my own megaphone, put on my uniform, and worked the other side of the stadium. Fortunately, the thousands of returning veterans were wedged into that area, so I had a huge cheering section all my very own.

Fortunately or unfortunately, my career as a cheerleader was about to come to a sudden stop. It was after the 13-7 win over Marquette. The cheerleaders today have PA systems. But all we had then were megaphones and voices. I yelled at the top of my lungs for the length of the game. I had since the third grade. And generally I lost my voice on Sunday and barely had it back on Monday. I arrived at our 8 a.m. "Adventures in Music" Monday morning rehearsal, and, as usual, most of my voice was left somewhere out on the football field.

J. Kenneth Richards gave me an ultimatum in front of the whole cast and rightly so. He was angry.

"Mr. Beals, you are going to have to make a decision. Are you in school to be a professional cheerleader or a professional radio actor?"

"Professional radio actor," was my weak, hoarse reply.

"That's what I thought you'd say. I won't let you hurt this

36

show. And your present condition hurts this show. You couldn't sing worth a lick and you know it."

I nodded sadly but knowingly. He turned on his heel and the others quickly cast their eyes on scripts, music, violins, fingernails, and whatever.

As I have repeatedly said, things happen for a reason. If only positive thoughts enter your subconscious, positive results will happen. Such was the case in my finally getting an opportunity to move into a dorm. Two radio majors were losing their roommate, so they asked me to move in. This meant getting special permission from the head of Campus Housing, because only returning veterans were allowed in dorms. Special permission was given, so spring term I moved in.

We were at dinner one evening and Art, Ernie and I were discussing a radio assignment which involved writing, producing, directing and acting in a 15-minute show. Another student was listening and eating with little or no interest. Then he dropped a bombshell.

"If it would help you guys, I know the announcer on the Lone Ranger show. I could set it up for us all to see one of their shows if you wanted to."

We all just looked at one another in disbelief. Ernie came to his senses first. "Just like that," he said as he snapped his fingers, "we could actually watch them do a show." Then clown that he was, he said, "Oh, I don't know if I could find time for something like that. Could you guys?"

"Yes!!!" we screamed in unison.

Between our bites our newfound friend said, "I'll call Harry Golder this weekend and set it up. We could leave right after classes on a Friday and make their 7:30 p.m. broadcast. Dick, why don't you check the bus schedules."

I did and Friday we all took off. Little did I know then what the future held for me. But I remember so clearly a feeling I had as we sat quietly in the clients area, just outside the studio. They had just gone on the air. Like a burst of freon gas, a chill went through me that gave me a shiver to end all shivers. It was really scary. I didn't know then what it meant, but I know now that *someone* was trying to tell me something.

It was a thrill to be there, though, just as if I were in a dream. I had been listening to this show since 1934. The voices were all so familiar. Listening and watching these pros told me one thing. I could hack this end of the business. And I belonged in dramatic radio. Dr. Robert J. Coleman was right. Now I just had to figure out how. I decided right then and there to listen carefully for Angel Voices. I knew they would be there when I needed them.

Golder was nice enough to introduce us all around, including 6'5" Brace Beamer, the Lone Ranger, 86-year-old John Todd who played Tonto, and veteran actors Rollie Parker, Ernie Winstanley, Jimmy Fletcher, Bill Saunders, Harry Goldstein and the director, a man named Charles D. Livingston. He joked that he was from the University of Michigan . . . and added with a wink and almost a smile, "But I decided to let you Spartans in anyway."

It was about that time that I wrote to Mr. Woodfill in Chicago and by return mail I received an invitation to return to Mackinac Island for the '48 season. I accepted immediately, knowing that I would need that money if I was to continue. At least I thought I would need it. It was hard to believe I was about to be a senior. Finals were a bit easier, especially in my major, but the spectre of still being a few credits short of graduating hung over my head. Having to leave a final exam due to food poisoning in my freshman year and the resultant F grade probably meant summer school in 1949. But that was light-years away. It was summertime and that meant a trip north to the Grand Hotel and a job. A paying job.

7

"Stay on Course, Young Man"

The summer turned out to be more profitable than the first one by about $250. I had plenty in the bank, almost $2,000. How beautifully life works when you let it! In the summer of '46 I barely had enough to complete my second year of college. A chance trip (chance by some people's definition) to Mackinac Island, turning the problem or rather the challenge over to a higher power for the solution, and now two years later having more money than I ever thought possible. I was actually working my way through college. THINK BIG.

Fall of 1948. My senior year. I knew going in I couldn't possibly graduate in June because of that dratted Literature and Fine Arts F. So I planned my schedule for the fall term with that in mind. Only fifteen credit hours, as many classes in my major as possible (I was allowed only 90 total), a continuation of my English writing courses, my history minor, journalism and something in PE, fly casting. Nothing too strenuous.

The fall term was well under way when a strange feeling began gnawing away at my insides. Call it fear or doubt or uncertainty. Whatever. But the thought hit me . . . hey, I'm a senior and next summer I will be out looking for work. What work? Where? Doing what? I'd never thought about it. My whole fight had been in seeking jobs and money to finish. Now what do I do?

So I sought out Dr. Robert Coleman, my mentor of three years before, and the man who promoted my acting ventures.

"Well, you are going to have to make a decision, Richard: acting or station management or advertising. I can't see you ever latching on as an announcer. Your voice is not what they are looking for. You will do well in either of the latter two, given time. But you belong in acting. And that means Chicago, New York, Hollywood."

"Yes, sir, but how?"

"By being there."

"Living there?"

"Yes."

"But I don't know anybody there." I was beginning to panic.

"You never do in this business. You didn't know anybody here three years ago and now look at you." With that he paused, looked at me with that warm fatherly look he had, took off his glasses, rubbed his eyes and I guess decided to say what he had in mind. It was to be words to live by.

"Keep your goal in mind. You will always know the right people. The right people will always find you and like you. It's one of the good things going for you. Do you understand what I'm trying to say?"

"Yes, sir. Thank you." I was getting a little choked up and so was he, although he was better at hiding it.

My dad was not the type to talk to me like this. He never would have been able to. Maybe Dr. Coleman couldn't talk to his kids either, but he was surely what the doctor ordered for me.

"Before you graduate take time to do your homework. Find out where all the radio shows are being done. Listen to them. Determine which shows use kids and how often. Compile names and addresses of directors, the show's sponsors, their ad agencies. Then give it a try. You know you can do the work, don't you?"

"Yes. I saw the Lone Ranger show last spring. I could do their show today with no problem."

"Then, young man, it's just a matter of saving your money and taking the gamble. OK?"

"OK."

He got up, signaling the end of the meeting. We shook hands and he added one more word of encouragement. "Let's talk some more. Keep me posted."

But first, I had to get my positive thinking in order. So I did. I knew I was an actor. I wanted to be paid for acting on radio. It was that simple. Let go and let God. And THINK BIG.

I turned it over completely. I went about my classes, life in the dorm, football games, radio shows at WKAR when they came up with no fear of the future whatsoever, keeping always that vision in front of me about acting professionally. It was a great feeling. I just knew everything was working out in my best interests. Also I kept it to myself. That's a rule we had learned at home.

I was wandering through the lobby of the dorm, trying to figure out how to get a ride home for Thanksgiving, when the student on the switchboard yelled that I had a call from home. This meant running back to our precinct to find an empty phone booth, which I did. It was mother.

"Have I got good news for you!"

"You mean a ride home? Is dad coming up?"

"No, no, no. This is about a job. Remember Jean Eddy? Well, she is working for an ad agency in Detroit called Wolfe, Jickling, Dow and Conkey and they have a TV show on WWJ called the Hudson Sketch Book. You know, the J.L. Hudson Company?"

"And they want me?" hoping she would get to the point sometime today.

"Well now, be quiet and let me tell you. Jean didn't have any idea where you were or what you were doing so she called here. I told her all about what you were doing and your acting experience. They are doing five Wednesday evening TV shows from Thanksgiving to Christmas about Santa Claus and his workshop and they need someone to play the part of Jumpy, Santa's little helper."

"For money?"

"Well, I didn't want to ask but I assume so. They want you in their office Saturday morning at 10 o'clock. I told them you'd be there."

"Well, I guess I can miss the game this Saturday."

"GAME! Of course you can miss a GAME. Catch a bus after your last class on Friday and get home here. Dad will take you down Saturday morning. He has to be at the General Motors Building but he'll drop you off first. Oh . . . and wear your best suit. Is your hair cut nice?"

"Yes, Mother," I said as insulted as I could sound. I guess in the eyes of your mother you never grow up.

I did take the bus home. I didn't wear my best suit because I didn't have one, but I did wear my best gray corduroy sports jacket with one of my two knit ties. Dad took me down to Detroit and I was there 15 minutes early, as usual. The agency office was closed so I had to wait in the hall. As 10:05 a.m. rolled around I thought no one would show up or I was at the wrong place, and I was getting itchy. Then the elevator doors opened and three folks came strolling casually down the hall carrying cardboard coffee cups and half-eaten doughnuts.

"You must be Dick Beals," said the man in the lead. "My name is Jim Clark. This is Pat Tobin and Don Irwin. Been waiting long?"

"No," I fibbed, "only a few minutes."

Clark found a key and opened the door to the darkened agency lobby, switched on some lights and led the way down a hall to his office, switching on more lights as he went. It was quite cold, which he also noticed.

"Get comfortable while I find the thermostat around here." And dumping his topcoat and briefcase and keys, he headed back down the hall.

The very pretty blonde model type started dumping her stuff, except for her box of Kleenex. It was obvious she had a cold.

"When did you come down from campus, Dick?" she asked sniffling into her Kleenex.

"Late afternoon yesterday after my four o'clock class. Got

41

the last bus to Birmingham."

"Senior?" asked the chunky Irwin.

"Yes."

Clark had returned by then and immediately took charge. He removed scripts from his brief case and he passed them out. "Dick, you're acquainted with the J. L. Hudson Company. We produce a weekly 15-minute TV show for them featuring items from their store. It's Detroit's first regularly scheduled television program. Pat is the hostess on the show. We thought it would be cute to have a Santa Claus theme from Thanksgiving to Christmas. And we thought it would be appropriate to have a little helper for Santa. That's you. Don will be Santa." He peered at me over his half glasses for some semblance of understanding, but I was just sitting there nodding. I was waiting for an opening to ask questions so I took it.

"How do you want me to play Jumpy other than bright and cheerful? Will he be playing tricks on Santa? Do you want him precocious, mischievous or seen but not heard?"

"OK, good point. Hadn't thought that much about it." Here he paused and looked at Pat, perhaps for an answer or just inspiration and she just continued to sniff.

"Well, let's just read it and see how it plays. Try it the way it feels to you and let me hear it."

It was a cute show. "Gail" came to visit us at Toy Town via a magic merry-go-round and we showed her the newest toys for kids. We also promoted the big Thanksgiving Day Parade that the J. L. Hudson Company had sponsored annually for years and years. My character supplied the only comic relief by disappearing all the time due to shyness and/or being a little rascal.

"Are you all comfortable with the script? Dick?"

"Yes, but I have a suggestion for the name of my character. If it isn't too late."

"What's that?"

"Jumpy connotes nervousness. Instead of Jumpy . . . how about Jump Jump?"

"Jump Jump," mused Santa, kind of tasting it.

"Jump Jump," coughed Pat. "That's cute."

"Yeah, I like it," smiled Jim. "Jump Jump! That's easier to say and that's how I want you to play him on the set. Kind of all over the place. Everywhere at once. Yeah . . . let's go with that. I like it."

We read through it again with Jim putting a clock on it this time. Of course it was long. Scripts are always long. He made some preliminary cuts. "All right, let's go with it this way, then time it after a run-through Wednesday. Now costumes. Don, you're set, so you can go. Dick, you stay, so we can take some measurements.''

They soon realized I was a size 10, took my waist measurement and a few others. Jim made some notes and tucked them in his briefcase.

"Now let's talk about the schedule and money, Dick. We're paying $50 a show. You'll do five of them. Read-through every Saturday at 10 a.m. Be at WWJ at 3 p.m. each Wednesday until further notice."

"I'll have to do some fast talking on campus but I'll be here. The money is OK but if you could throw in something for transportation and food I'd appreciate it. I may have to take the train if the bus isn't available. I'll have to check."

"OK . . . you just give me your costs each Wednesday and I'll include it in that week's check. How's that?"

"That would really help. I'm going to school on a tight budget and every little bit will help."

He reached across his desk to shake hands. "Great to have you aboard, Dick. You are really going to help us. See you Wednesday."

"See you, honey," echoed Pat. "You were great. We're really going to have fun with this. See you Wednesday."

I left their office 10 feet high. Fifty bucks! Live TV! Acting! Talk about being thrilled. I couldn' t believe it. Thank you, Jean Eddy, wherever you are. I left the big office building and started walking toward the station to catch a bus to the General Motors Building, only to hear a shy, little beep of a car horn. There was Old Dependable, my dad, with engine running, waiting at the curb.

He could tell when I jumped in I was thrilled to pieces. But as usual he drove in total silence. He wasn't much at conversation.

"Well, I got the part."

He lit a cigarette. There was silence except for a quiet "hmmmmm" exhaling his smoke.

"I'm getting $50 a show plus food and transportation."

"Transportation? What transportation? That's peanuts."

"To me it's a lot of money. I may have taxi fares, may have to take a train. I didn't know what that would cost. I had only two seconds to think so I asked."

Silence. Then, "How many shows?"

"Five. Script read-through each Saturday at 10 a.m., WWJ at 3 p.m. on Wednesday."

"How about your classes?"

"That'll be tough. I'll have to talk to my counselor on Monday. They'll have to help me somehow. This is just too darned important. It isn't often a senior gets a job like this while he's still in school. In fact it is NEVER. They'll help me somehow.''

8

The Budding Actor Gets a Break

"OK, let's do this," began Dr. Buell, genuinely excited at the good news. "Go see your professors today and explain the situation to them. Ask them to call me. We'll work out something."

So I did. They were cooperative. As long as they knew when I would be missing the class and why, they agreed to accept late papers, assignments, speeches or whatever.

Wednesday finally got there, and despite the bus being a bit late, I arrived at WWJ 10 minutes early. The receptionist checked a list and, finding my name on it, directed me to the second-floor studio.

Jim Clark saw me coming out of the elevator and motioned me into the studio where they were putting the final touches on the set.

"You made it on time I see. No problems?"

"Oh, the bus was late, what with the Thanksgiving holiday, but things worked out OK."

"Well, here's the set. What do you think? Does it look like Toy Town?"

"I'm impressed. Will this be our set for all five shows?"

"All five. Just different toys. Oh, let's go find your costume and try it on. The seamstress from Hudson's is standing by just in case there's a problem."

Finding the dressing room, such as it was, I tried the costume on and to everyone's amazement it fit just fine. I said "such as it was" because in 1948 television was quite new and this had formerly been just a radio studio where dressing rooms were not needed. In fact Ty Tyson's office was about 30 feet from the "Dressing Room," which I felt sure had been a supply room. Anyway I thought the costume fit fine, but the seamstress found some imperfections which she fixed while we were rehearsing.

Jim had us walk through it. I was amazed—no, shocked— that Gail and Santa didn't know their lines. I couldn't imagine professionals would come to the set unprepared. But I had learned one thing years ago from a sixth grade teacher while doing Tom Sawyer. Never, never feed another actor a line during rehearsals. It is considered very bad manners. Let the director do it. During the actual performance either feed it or cover for it. But only then. That lesson would come home to roost during the last show.

We rehearsed and rehearsed. We had to be able to work the

45

toys perfectly, and the toys had to work perfectly. This was really a 15-minute commercial. The head buyer from the toy department was there along with reps from the manufacturers to ensure that everything would work. We were well trained.

Jim was pleased, so before the dress rehearsal he took us all to dinner at a local coffee shop. Talk about being hungry. Breakfast had been my last meal.

For the dress rehearsal I got into my costume, someone put some makeup on me, which I still hated from early Jam Handy days, and we did a pretty good dress. Jim made some corrections, more cuts, changed some stage directions and told us to relax 'til airtime.

Then came Jim's "30 seconds" call and suddenly we were on the air. The 15 minutes seemed like 15 seconds. It was a blur. The show went as rehearsed, even better. It was crisper, probably from the touch of nervousness or trying harder or whatever. By airtime Santa and "Gail" had their lines down pat, the toys worked perfectly and Jim was ecstatic.

"Good job, Jump Jump," he said patting me on the back. "Right on the money. That's a real nice character you've developed."

I didn't know what to say so I didn't say anything except thanks and I-think-I'll-go-get-the-costume-and-the-makeup-off.

On the way out Pat also said some nice things along with the camera guys on the floor and the floor manager. It sounded nice but I had learned long ago they say that even if you've done a bad job. The only proof is getting the next call.

If I had any doubt I was in my right place I soon knew it, for sure. After our next Saturday rehearsal, Jim brought up a new subject at lunch.

"Dick, how easy is it for you to get into town for work?"

"Classes are no problem, or at least not a major problem. The instructors know what I'm doing and are all for it. So it's just a matter of knowing in advance and getting here."

"Have you ever heard of our Mark Adams Show?"

"No."

"Weekly radio show, half hour, adventure type. And we could use you. We have an awful time getting kids that can act and you'd really be able to help us."

"I'm, uh, well, I'm ready. I love radio. I'm honored."

"This will help our writers considerably. The client wants kids involved in the stories so I'll tell them to start writing you in."

I just stopped eating and stared into space. I couldn't believe what I was hearing.

"Something wrong with your lunch, honey?"

"No, Pat, everything's fine. Living in two different worlds

gets me to thinking sometime." And thinking I was—about missing classes, bus rides, how was I going to graduate in June with my class, how could I make up the missing credits, why hadn't I passed that Literature and Fine Arts course. Jim's next line brought me back to reality in a hurry.

"By the way, an actor named Bill Saunders plays Mark Adams. He's anxious to meet you. He was saying last week that they are having the same problem of finding kids on the other shows he does."

"Boy, will I be anxious to see him."

"He was telling the director about you. A man named Charles Livingston . . ."

"The director on the Lone Ranger show?" I asked, interrupting him and almost choking on my sandwich.

"And the Green Hornet and the Challenge of the Yukon. All network shows. You'd be in good company."

With that I just grinned and shook my head in disbelief. What a moment. These were some of the top shows on the air.

"I don't know when the first script will be coming up but it might be before Christmas. I'll know more Wednesday."

I vaguely remember the walk back to the bus station. I do know that I got my ticket and ran to get near the beginning of the line and in a front-row seat. The ride home was a good-news-bad-news kind of ride. The future looked bright. I had a shot at network radio, live TV, local radio and who knows what else. But how could I get out of school in June needing 41 credits? Then I took another tack and the right tack. Why it wasn't my first thought I'll never know. The law says . . . if *one* thing has worked out OK, *everything* has worked out OK. And worked out OK for everyone. So, dummy, let go of this thing, relax, turn it over, and keep moving forward in a positive way. THINK BIG!

Everyone at school pitched in and solved my problem. Dean of Students Tom King talked to my professors, and they agreed to assist me in every way possible. I was allowed to take 21 credits in winter term and 20 in spring term, all snap courses. I could attend when I could and do my best with the work load. I was virtually promised a passing grade in each course.

But my toughest challenge awaited me when I arrived early for rehearsal for the final show. Jim was waiting for me as I walked into the studio. There was an older man with him.

"Dick, hi. Glad you're early. Meet Stan Howard. He's going to be Santa tonight."

"Mr. Howard, nice to meet you."

Mr. Howard nodded and ignored my outstretched hand.

"OK, team, let's use the set here and walk through this thing."

Jim blocked it, reading Gail's lines. It was obvious that Howard didn't know his. But I excused this, thinking he was a last-minute replacement and had just gotten the script. That is, until Jim mentioned something referring to Saturday's read-through, from which I had been excused because of finals. Then I realized that Howard just hadn't bothered to memorize his lines or he was a slow learner.

Remembering the rule about never feeding a fellow actor lines, I just let him suffer and stammer and sneak peaks at his script. He tried to take out his frustrations on me, of course, but Jim was right there, so he held back the best he could. The whole thing caused me to learn his lines and actions as if I would be a stand-in. It was going to be a real learning situation.

Two rehearsals later it was still a bit rough but we still had a dress to do so I was hopeful. His roughest part was in demonstrating a new record called a 45. We were introducing them for the first time on this show. He was having a rough time tying in the lines and the demonstration. And he was blaming it all on me, making up excuses that were somehow my fault. Needless to say, I sneaked back when he was gone and practiced his part about 20 times just in case he blew it. RCA would never have forgiven us.

He really blew up at me just before the dress. We were both in the small room where we put on our costumes and whatever makeup we wore. Howard was fussing and fuming about forgetting his white hair cover-up for his natural brown sideburns and mustache. Jim was there trying to settle him down.

"No, Jim. I'm sorry. Santa will just have to have a brown mustache and brown sideburns. There's no time to go out and get some cover-up. No one will ever notice anyway."

"Stan, now calm down. First of all *I* will notice. And second, we'll figure out something. Let me go out and see if they have a makeup man coming in for any reason tonight."

"Lousy, cheap outfit," Howard ranted and raved like a spoiled kid. "TV just doesn't respect the professional actor. No makeup people, no dressing rooms. This stinks."

Major decision time. I had a suggestion, even a solution. But as a novice and the new kid on the block I was brought up not to say anything. Before I knew it I just blurted it out.

"Use this, Mr. Howard." I was holding out to him some plain old ordinary toothpaste. I always carried it in my topcoat when I traveled, along with my toothbrush.

"What's that?"

"Toothpaste. We use it at school all the time in our drama classes."

"Toothpaste? Are you kidding? That's the dumbest thing I've

ever heard. Sorry, kid. Nice try. But you've got a lot to learn in this business. Better stay in school a few more years."

I was about to become unprofessional for a minute and get angry but decided to keep quiet. About 10 minutes later Jim came charging in out of breath with a brown paper bag full of something.

"OK, I talked to the makeup man. He told me to go to the drugstore and get this for you. He uses it all the time." And two guesses what Jim pulled out of the brown paper bag. Tee hee.

"What's this crap?" snarled Howard.

"Colgate toothpaste," smiled Jim.

I exited as quickly as possible. But with one parting shot. As I passed Jim at the door I mumbled, "Great idea, Jim."

From that point on Howard was impossible. In the "dress" he was lost. He was so wrapped up in his misery and bad attitude that he forgot lines and blew cues and ran right over my lines. At the break I cornered Jim. "What do you want me to do? This could be a disaster."

"Do you know his lines?"

I nodded.

"Can you do his demos?"

I nodded. He looked off into the distance somewhere and for a long time. "OK, be ready to cover for him. But don't make it obvious."

"OK."

I went back to the set and ran through the toys, the sales points, the colors (this was black-and-white, remember), the prices and all the other items we were featuring on that show. It was good that I did.

The show as it was written and rehearsed bore little resemblance to the show we did. Howard just plain froze. Gail filled in for him at first, but then it was just the two of us, Jump Jump and Santa, on live TV, as we demonstrated the sponsor's key Christmas sales items. It began with the new 45 RPM records.

Santa was supposed to say something like, "Well, Jump Jump, look at these new 45 RPM records."

And Jump Jump was supposed to ask: "What's a 45 RPM, Santa?"

Santa: "Well, Jump Jump" . . . and then he goes into his pitch. But Santa couldn't remember which product came next.

So Jump Jump, that clever fellow, "jumped" in with, "Golly, Santa, here's something new, a 45 RPM record." And holding the stack of records up so I could look at him *and* the camera through the new, larger hole, I added, "And look how the

49

center area is thicker so that the grooves don't touch." Then I held them up horizontally and looked through the spaces. Then he was supposed to ask if I would like to play one on the record player with the large spindle adapter, but he didn't.

Jump Jump: "Santa, could we play one? I'd like to see how the spindle adapter works." He nodded. Thank goodness he remembered how.

The whole show went like that. I had to cue him and practically read him into almost every line he had. I was hoping and praying that the sponsor wasn't at home following along with the script. He could very well think it was I who was messing up or trying to hog the show or whatever. I was also concerned for the Jump Jump character being out of character by being so much in charge.

But Jim had said GO! And after all, he would be the final authority. I hoped.

When Santa said his final line, which he pulled off without a hitch, and we could see on the monitor that we were off the air, Santa Claus, with his costume, toothpaste and all, headed for the North Pole. Not a word to anyone. Just a dirty look at me over his shoulder. I was exhausted and confused, and I guess I showed it. Then something happened that brought me to my senses. The crew started to applaud. Then Pat came on the set and was applauding. And I was just standing there with tears in my eyes shaking my head in amazement.

Pat was hugging me saying, "Nice job, young man. You saved the show, and probably the series."

Jim was shaking my hand. His face was a mass of perspiration and his shirt was soaking wet. "I just talked to the sponsor. He was at home following the script and wondered what was going on. I told him. He was very grateful. I know you have a time problem. Go get out of your costume and makeup. I'll give you a ride to the bus station."

We didn't have much to say during the short ride to the station. But as I got out he handed me an envelope.

"Compliments of the J. L. Hudson Company and Wolfe, Jickling, Dow and Conkey and Merry Christmas. We think you deserve a bonus."

I opened it. It was a check for $150. "One-hundred-fifty dollars! One-hundred-fifty dollars! For me?"

"That's $50 for Jump Jump, $50 for also playing Santa and $50 bonus. Plan on seeing a lot of us next year." He drove off with a big wave out the window and I just stood there. What a day. What an experience. Merry Christmas and Happy 1949.

9

Dreams Do Come True

Winter term was a pistol. Courses coming out of my ears, meetings with Dr. King, Dr. Buell, professors, and instructors, and stacks and stacks of books. Thank goodness everyone went along with the plan.

Some of the courses were a real waste. One professor never took roll, lectured the whole period and never gave exams. He had a Henry-Kissinger-type voice and no one could understand him. The class tried though. Every once in a while he would finish a sentence and grin from ear to ear. This was our cue to laugh like crazy and he would be so pleased he'd pick up his notes, close his notebook and leave. He didn't seem to notice the period still had 30 minutes left to go.

Wolfe, Jickling, Dow and Conkey (known in the industry as Wolf, Chicken, Cow and Donkey), were thinking of me too. Jim called the dorm during lunch one day.

"Can you handle a radio show and a TV show in one day?"

"I guess so. Both at WWJ?"

"Yes, and I'll schedule it to get you on that last bus at 9:06 p.m. Can you get here by noon?"

"I'm sure there's an early bus or early train. I'll do it somehow."

"OK, if there's a problem get back to me, pronto. OK?"

"I'll be there. What's the TV show?"

"Same show but this time you're a kid that asks a million questions about new bikes, skis, toboggans, sleds and the clothes that go with them. What size do you wear?"

"Ten. Waist 28."

"Well, you won't need special pants in this, just shirts, sweaters and jackets. Just wear your normal school clothes. Do you ski?"

"I know the basics. I ski a bit around here on little, safe hills."

"OK. The radio show will be in the afternoon. It's the Mark Adams Show. Kid's part. For a pro like you it'll be a snap."

"Yeah, a pro. Five 15-minute TV shows. What a career. But thanks."

"OK, big guy, see you next Wednesday, 12 noon unless I hear from you. OK? I'll have a sandwich waiting for you."

"Yes, sir. Next Wednesday." I grabbed the phone book and called the Greyhound Station. They had an 8 a.m. bus that would make it in time. And Jim was right. The 9:06 bus got me back to school about 11:30 p.m. Long day, but this was what I had asked for and had received.

The show was easy but once again I kept pinching myself. I couldn't believe I was actually doing a radio show, with pros, and getting paid for it. But bless J. Kenneth Richards and Michigan State . . . they had trained all of us well. Bill Saunders was impressed too.

"Still in school, Jim tells me. How do you get out of class?" I explained the situation.

"I'll be doing the Ranger show tomorrow. I know Chuck Livingston would be interested in you. How do we get in touch with you?"

On the back of the script's title sheet I wrote my dorm number and my number in Birminghan. "If you can't get me at the dorm call my house in Birmingham. My mother will get me. She has my schedule."

"OK, I'll pass this along to Chuck. We'll see what happens."

And that's all he said. The show went well. My part called for a bit of crying and screaming and generally a bratty kid so it gave me a chance to act. I was hoping it impressed Saunders.

So it was out one door, down the hall and into Studio A. We went right into a rehearsal. Everyone had their lines down pat, which is as it should be, so we moved along quickly.

The show went well, compared to the last one with the inept Santa.

It was a mad dash to the bus station, but after 15 minutes I was sound asleep all curled up on my seat with my topcoat over me. Next thing I knew I felt a nudge, and woke up with the driver trying to get my attention.

"Here's the campus, kid. Where do you want to get off?"

"About two blocks more, where the dorms start. That'll be a big help. I live just one block over."

So he stopped at just the right spot, swung the big door open and I jumped out into the freezing January weather. It was 11:45 p.m. I had started out at 6 a.m. It was 86 miles down, 86 miles back, a live TV show, a recorded radio show, and not much in the way of relaxed dining or quality food. I had a 9 a.m. class in English writing. I wasn't adequately prepared. But now I was a professional actor and it went with the territory. For the first time I had to use my special key to get into the dorm. They locked up at 11 o'clock. I tiptoed down the hall and slipped quietly into my room. Sleep came quickly.

About a week later there was a message in my box to call home. It was mother who answered the phone.

"A Mr. Saunders called. Do you know him?"

"Sure, he's Mark Adams on that show I did last week. Why was he calling you?"

"He said he lost your note and got our number from Wolfe, Jickling whatever it is."

"Well, why didn't you give him my number?"

"Because I told him I'd take charge of it and call you."

"Well, I'd rather have him call me direct. It's simpler that way. Did he say what he wanted?"

"Certainly he did. And I am quite capable of taking these calls, young man."

"What did he want, Mother? This is a long-distance call and I'm in a phone booth, and in a few seconds I'm going to have to start feeding nickels into this thing."

"Well, then be quiet and let me talk. I'm in charge of this one. He wanted to know if you'd be interested in doing a commercial on the Challenge of the Yukon show, whatever that is."

"Really?"

"So I told him I didn't think you'd be willing to do *just* a commercial . . . ."

"YOU WHAT?"

"Certainly! I told him that's a long way to come just for a commercial . . . ."

Click. "This is the Operator . . . please deposit another 25¢ for three minutes . . . ."

Clang, clang, clang, clang, clang.

"Mother, tell me you're kidding. What are you trying to do? Do you know what a break this is for me?"

"Is it a big show?"

"A BIG SHOW!!? Live, network. A chance to work on the Lone Ranger, Green Hornet, Challenge of the Yukon. Holy cow, *just* a commercial. What's the matter with you?"

"Well, it didn't hurt to ask. All he could do was say no."

"Say NO? How did you leave it? When is it?"

"Now don't get excited. I'll call him and tell him OK. I was only trying to get you more money."

"Mother, no one gets more money. It's scale."

"Well, I didn't know that."

"That's what I mean. I'm an unknown. I'm trying my darndest to get a start in this business, and you're playing games in something you know nothing about."

"Well, I'll call him back then and say it's OK."

"No, let me call him. I'll explain to him you didn't understand the situation . . . ."

Click. "This is the operator. Please deposit another 25¢ for an additional three minutes."

Clang, clang, clang, clang, clang.

"No, I'll call him. Let me be important for once. I was just trying to help. It didn't hurt to try."

"MOTHER-R-R-R."

"It's for Friday . . . this week, WXYZ Studios, East Jefferson at Iroquois. Be there at 4 p.m. Mr. Saunders will introduce you to Mr. Fred Flowerday, the director. Ask for him in the lobby."

By now my head was going *Clang, clang, clang.* "What's his number, Mother?"

"Never mind. I'll call him. It's my turn to be in charge. I'll call you right back if it isn't OK."

"No. Call me back if it *is* OK. And Mother . . . ."

"Now what?"

"No tricks. Just tell him I was overjoyed at being asked and I'll be there early. Understand?"

"Oh, for crying out loud, you act as if I don't know anything. I was once a professional artist, remember!"

"Yes, Mother. Call him and get right back. I'm running out of quarters."

"All right. All right. Don't worry. I'll handle Mr. Saunders. Goodbye."

I wanted to bust up the phone booth or the nearest wall, but they were both bigger than I was. "Handle Mr. Saunders" indeed! I made it upstairs to the office where the switchboard was located and let the operator know I was expecting a long-distance call. In about five minutes the buzzer sounded, and the outside trunk lighted up.

"Phillips Hall. Yes, just a minute please." He nodded at me.

I ran down to my precinct for the nearest phone booth. It was my "agent."

"Well, it's OK. I told him you'd be there. See, I told you it would be all right."

"I'll be there. But after this . . . give them my number, please."

"Oh, you take yourself too seriously. It's only a commercial. Will you come home for the weekend?"

"I wasn't planning on it but now I'll have to. See you when I see you. And that's 4 p.m. at WXYZ, East Jefferson at Iroquois. What a break. I can't wait."

"Well, be good. Bye."

Friday was there like a shot. The nicely dressed lady at the front desk in the huge foyer of the WXYZ studios, once a fashionable, top-drawer mansion, was expecting me and even called me by name. She said that Bill Saunders was expecting me.

I could hear heavy footsteps coming up a flight of stairs from somewhere, and then out through a door towards the back of the entry hall came the burly ex-cop, Mr. Saunders. He was all smiles. "Always early, aren't you, young man?"

"Thanks to an on-time bus and a knowledgeable taxi driver."

"Well, good to see you. Come on in and meet Fred Flower-day, the director. We're on a break now. We'll do a dress in about 15 minutes. We air at 5 p.m."

We went back through that same door and into the clients area where all of us sat for the Ranger show about a year ago.

Fred Flowerday was in the booth. He was younger than Mr. Livingston, wore glasses and looked athletic and in shape.

"Fred, Dick Beals is here."

Dropping whatever he was doing he grabbed a script and headed down the steps out of the booth, once the kitchen, right hand outstretched.

"Dick, nice to meet you. We've heard a lot about you from Bill. Just get in?"

"Yes, sir. Good to be here. It's a real thrill."

"Great. Let's go into the studio and get you something to stand on. That mike's pretty high. I want you to read this through a couple of times with our announcer. Bill, would you see if Jay could come up?"

"Sure."

"Here's your script." Fred handed me one page of copy as he led me into the carpeted, draped, softly lighted 20x20 studio, probably the living room in days of yesteryear. It was obvious the single mike was set for six-footers. It had a four-foot-high wooden stool placed under it. "Play him about 10. Bright. Sharp. Cute." He kept walking trying to get an idea of something I could stand on and I followed, anxious to see everything. We went to the sound room, which at first glance appeared to be full of junk, but the junk was paraphernalia used by sound men to create sounds. The largest items were two big, waist-high, shallow boxes filled with areas of sand, rock, stones and dirt. Sitting in there were four half coconut shells with straps fitted over the tops. When placed on the hands of a sound effects man and pounded into the dirt, they sound like horses' hoofs.

There were the usual doors set in frames that were on wheels, strawberry boxes and wads of cellophane for fire sounds, spurs to jingle and a myriad of gimmicks used for the three shows.

Fred was digging over in the corner and came up with a small box about 12 inches high and 15 inches long.

"This is an old ammo case. Let's try this."

Back in the studio we went, Fred with an old towel trying to wipe off my new riser. Now there was another man there, cigarette in hand, rather rotund, balding, clipped mustache, reminding me slightly of a young Oliver Hardy, of Laurel and Hardy fame.

"Dick Beals, this is Jay Michael, our announcer."

We shook hands and exchanged greetings. "Dick is up at Michigan State and is here to do the kid on the middle spot. Let's run it through once for levels. Dick, you work on the other side of the mike from Jay. Keep the box out of the way until the middle break, then push it into place. When you're finished, take it out of there and put it under that bench over there in the corner."

With that he rushed out, closed the door and jumped up into the elevated director's area. The engineer was standing down in front of him getting switches and levers set up.

There were small brass handles on each end of the case so I practiced hauling it around, which was quite easy. It appeared to be old and not too solid. I figured it was World War I, not II.

"OK, let's try one. When you're ready, Jay."

The magnificent, professionally trained and very familiar voice came on smooth. Out of the corner of my eye I noticed someone had joined Bill Saunders outside in the clients area. It was Charles D. Livingston himself. "Only a commercial" was, in actuality, my audition. I read my lines, holding my script and head up as high as possible to make sure I was square on mike. I didn't hold back. I gave it my best shot.

At the end, Jay winked at me and mouthed the word "good." Livingston had now moved to the door of the booth and was saying something to Fred.

"OK, Dick, let's try it again and see what happens if you play him older, about 13-14."

I looked up at him and nodded through the glass. "When you're ready, guys."

Jay looked at me. I nodded. We went through it again.

"Any trouble sustaining that level, Dick?"

"No, sir."

Another confab between Fred and Mr. Livingston. "One more time then, and this time try him about five or six. OK, Dick?"

"Sure. The lines aren't written for a kid that young but I'll try it."

We did it again. It was difficult getting some of the words out playing him that young, so I cheated just a bit in places.

Jay was laughing when we finished. "That was cute," he said in a barely audible voice.

"Fine, Dick. Play him the way you did the first time. That'll work just fine. Are you comfortable with it?"

"Yes, sir."

"Is the riser OK?"

"Fine. Works fine." I moved it back under the bench and sat down.

Bill Saunders stuck his head inside the door as Jay was moving out. "Dick, can you come here a minute?" He held the door open for me and there stood Mr. Livingston. I didn't know if he remembered me or not.

"Dick, this is Mr. Livingston, our head director. This is Dick Beals, Chuck."

A cold, weak handshake greeted me. The watery eyes behind the thick glasses were looking me over very carefully.

"That was good work in there. We're very pleased."

"Thank you, sir. It's a thrill to be here."

"We also do the Lone Ranger and Green Hornet here, you know."

"Yes, Mr. Saunders told me. I was here about a year ago with some friends from school. Mr. Golder invited us. Little did I know then I'd be back."

"Oh yes, I kind of remember that. Mr. Golder is no longer with us. Fred Foy is the Ranger announcer now." He seemed to be getting uncomfortable with small talk so Bill jumped in.

"Dick, how about some coffee?"

"Yes, that would taste good."

Livingston wasn't finished, however. "Any trouble getting down here for shows."

"No. I've made the necessary arrangements with the dean and the profs. They understand how important it is to a senior to be able to do what he was trained to do."

Without a word Mr. Livingston abruptly left and headed for the lobby.

When everyone arrived in the studio, Bill introduced me all around as quickly as he could. I sat down on the bench guarding my ammo case and waited my turn. It was unbelievable sitting there listening to this collection of voices. They were good.

Bill had gotten me a script so I could follow along. As my spot came up I got the riser in hand and stood ready to move in. Ernie Winstanley, a cast regular, moved too quickly for me and almost tripped over it. I jerked it out of the way, just as he saw it. He patted me on the head with a big smile.

"Need any help?" he whispered. I shook my head no.

Jay and I did the spot. I hustled the box out of the way and slipped it under the bench. I glanced at Flowerday just as he was looking at me. He flashed me the OK sign with his hand. When Jay finished his lead into the second half, he came by and squeezed my shoulder and winked.

They all took the dress seriously, which meant to me the director took it seriously. There was a 15-minute break before Challenge of the Yukon airtime, so I just stayed in the studio and went over my lines. As everyone wandered back in, I took my spot on the bench with my ammo case.

I was ready to move in with my ammo case well in advance. Everyone else left the mike at the first-half break, leaving me plenty of time to get ready. In fact, Ted Johnstone, who played the part of King, Sergeant Preston's dog, gave me a big sweep of his hand and long, low bow as if to usher me in. Jay smiled at me and winked just before he turned to get his cue from Fred. And, just like we rehearsed it, we did it. Even better, I thought. Live, ABC network, coast to coast. Fortunately, that last thought didn't hit me until I had grabbed my riser and parked it under my bench and sat down.

Just then I noticed for the first time that Charles D. Livingston was in the clients area. I'm glad I hadn't noticed him before I did the spot. I was hoping to see even the smallest indication but he didn't even look at me. And soon thereafter I got so engrossed in the show that I forgot about everything. Needless to say, I didn't move a muscle. Some of the actors were nice enough to give me some sort of congratulatory reaction. A squeeze of the shoulder, an OK sign, a silent applause, a wink. It was very nice of them.

When the show was over I tucked the ammo case under the bench in the corner, just in case, and headed for the director's booth and Fred Flowerday. He was just packing things up and coming down out of his perch. "Thank you, young man. Very nice."

"Oh, thank you. I enjoyed it."

Just then Mr. Livingston came back in with some papers. "If you are finished with Mr. Beals, Fred, I have to get him to sign some stuff so he can get paid."

Fred and I shook hands, I thanked him profusely and then I followed Mr. Livingston out to the lobby and the now empty reception desk. "Sit down here and fill these things out where indicated. I'll be right back." He went up the long staircase as I went to work. In two minutes I was finished just as he came down the stairs. I was beginning to wonder if he ever smiled. He must have been in pain from something.

He checked over my work, put it into a file folder and then gave me a piece of paper with what looked like some instructions typed on it. "We like your work. We can use you. So I want you to do what everyone else does here. It's all on these instructions. Call me every Friday at 12 noon at that number. I will be waiting for your call. I'll give you your calls for the following week. You don't have to call if you are going to be here on Friday for either a Yukon or a Ranger. I'll give it to you in person then. You understand all that?"

"Got it. Thanks for giving me a shot. It was a real thrill."

"All right, you call me Friday then. Twelve noon." And he left for the studio and the Lone Ranger dress rehearsal. There I was, all alone in this deserted foyer, excited as all get-out and no one to talk to. About then Bill Saunders peeked in and, seeing me quite alone, hurried in with hand outstretched.

"Nice job, my boy. I'm proud of you. You really impressed the man." He then spotted my instructions and said, "Hey, now that's great. Welcome aboard."

"I sure appreciate what you did, Mr. Saunders."

"Bill, please."

"I have only one question."

"What's that?"

"How do I get a taxi to downtown?"

He really let loose a roar and gave me a big hug. "Come with me. Let's see if anyone is going that way." I followed him out to the stairway leading to the basement, and he shouted down the stairs, "Anyone heading downtown?"

"Yeah, I am," said an unrecognizable voice.

"Can you drop Dick off somewhere near the bus station?"

"Sure."

"Harry Goldstein will take you. I'm in the next show. Gotta hurry. Maybe see you next week, huh?"

"Hope so. Thanks again."

Harry Goldstein, the veteran actor, soon came up the stairs and we were on our way. He went out of his way to get me to the station. As I got out grabbing textbooks and notebooks and thanking him again, he looked me right in the eye and summed it all up pretty well: "This was a big day for you, Dick. You have quite a future ahead of you. Work hard."

"Thanks. I will. I promise." With that he waved and drove off. I climbed aboard Cloud Nine to Birmingham.

10
Double Life Is a Killer

Carrying 21 credits was tough enough but waiting for Friday noon was sheer agony. But a double life was what I had prayed for and received, so THINK BIG.

Mr. Livingston kept me busy. After my audition, of sorts, came several Challenge of the Yukon shows and then my first Lone Ranger. Thinking back to our group visit and then finding myself actually doing the show, I realized why I felt that chill of excitement watching it. Someone was trying to tell me something.

Another Friday noon finally arrived, and Mr. Livingston gave me my calls for the next week, or call rather. It was for another Lone Ranger show and it came close to being my last. My part was small on this particular show but I had the opening scene with John Todd, Tonto, Brace Beamer, the Lone Ranger, and actors Rollie Parker and Paul Hughes. Everything was routine during rehearsals. My ammo case, as usual, was either at the corner or beside the stool.

As we assembled for the broadcast I noticed my riser had been placed on Brace's side of the mike, at one corner of the stool. I asked Rollie why it had been moved and he just shrugged and said, "I guess that's where Livingston wants it."

Airtime approached and Brace, as usual, entered at 7:29:30. He sat on his bench, reviewed his script and got set for the opening scene. Fred was doing the commercial, the theme came up and he read us into the first scene. Brace had the first line, then I was to be next. He came to the mike, and not seeing the riser he cracked his shins on it. In a fit of temper he kicked it and it shattered into splinters. I kept trying to read my lines while jumping as high as I could to reach the mike, and I wasn't making it.

The director was glaring at me in disbelief. He didn't know what had happened to the ammo case. Rollie looked all over to find something quick but there was nothing.

Finally in desperation I grabbed the stool between lines and bumping people on the other side out of the way I climbed the rungs and with Rollie supporting me from behind, we finished the scene. Brace's magnanimous reaction to my problem: he glowered and rubbed his shins.

As soon as the show was over Rollie dashed into the control room and explained to Livingston what had happened. He knew that the Man didn't give people a second chance.

We had about 30 seconds between shows so the soundmen quickly found another box somewhere. Believe me, it stayed on the other side of the mike. After the show all Livingston said was, "Quick thinking." Beamer never did say anything.

Livingston handled the problem in a different way. My next call was for a Yukon two weeks later. As was my practice now, I immediately went downstairs to get a script and check in with Flowerday. A couple of them had funny grins on their faces but I didn't suspect anything.

When rehearsal time came we all went upstairs together, with me about in the middle of the throng. The studio was dark. I was about 10 feet inside the door when the lights went on. There, perched on top of the stool with a big green ribbon around it was a set of steps, about 15 inches wide and 15 inches high at the top step. It was painted green and white, with my name on the side. They had even carpeted the steps. I was over-whelmed and the others were cheering and laughing and applauding. Flowerday was their spokesman.

"Dick, just promise us you'll keep your steps on your side of the mike." More laughter and handshakes all around. If there had been any doubt in my mind that I belonged, it was long gone. It was a nice touch. Have no doubt, I stayed on the south side of that mike from that point on . . . three years' worth.

11

Go West, Young Man, It's Warmer

My double life continued. Some weeks nothing but school. Then two weeks of shows and bus rides.

The practical joker of the acting group was Ernie Winstanley. As I was the new actor I was on his hit list. Fortunately for me, veterans like Rollie, knowing the long days I faced, went out of their way to protect me. One day in particular. I had two shows, Yukon and Ranger, and that made for a long, long stress-filled day. Just before airtime, Rollie came to me and asked if I would hold onto Mr. Winstanley's script for him. "And put your script in your hip pocket, why don't you." Then he added, "When he comes in and asks you for it, give it to him, OK?"

I nodded OK.

Sure enough about 30 seconds before airtime Ernie struts in, spots me and comes over to where I'm sitting. "Hey kid," he said with great authority, "Can I see that script?"

"Sure, Mr. Winstanley, here."

With that he takes all 30 pages, removes the paper clip and throws them as hard as he can at the ceiling. Pages flutter all over the studio . . . wall to wall.

Laughing loudly he says, "OK, kid, there's your script. Find page one 'cause you have the first scene."

With that I pulled out my script from my hip pocket and said innocently, "Here's my script . . . that's yours."

Everyone was in on it except Mr. Winstanley and me. The rest of the cast was hiding behind draperies, behind each other, or heading for the sound room in uncontrolled laughter. At that moment, with Ernie on his hands and knees picking up pages, we heard the William Tell Overture beginning and poor Fred Foy trying not to break up reading, ". . . and from out of the past come the thundering hoof beats of the great horse Silver, the Lone Ranger." And there was Brace cupping his ear and shouting, "Hi Yo Silver, Away-y-y," and we were on the air. And Ernie was on his knees.

It was about late April or early May that the schedule started getting to me, physically. Headaches appeared on the scene for the first time in my life. I was tired much of the time. School wasn't fun. I couldn't wait to get out. The money I was making was incredible, considering I was working part time. The shows paid $56 as I remember, which was a lot of money. The bank account was building up quickly. But I still hurt a lot and began counting the days until I had my last class.

Graduation day finally came but I didn't bother to go to the formal ceremony. I just couldn't tolerate one more bus ride.

Now a new life began. One I hadn't counted on. Sure it was easier from a transportation standpoint. But I hadn't been living at home for four years. I had been independent and working and studying. I was now a boarder.

The one thing I had not figured on was the spare time I suddenly had without school or long bus rides. Two shows a week is nothing when you're home and zero shows a week means a lot of spare time. I started meditating on it and asked my Angels to go to work. Something worked out more quickly than I had anticipated.

Walking home the short two blocks from town I stopped to see our old family friend Russ McBride. Russ was just starting up a builders' hardware store after being in the general retail hardware business for years. As we finished our conversation he kiddingly asked me if I wanted to do some typing for him and I kiddingly said that I would. So he kiddingly showed me a huge pile of hardware schedules and some typing paper and said, "Fine, here. Original and one carbon."

So just to carry out our gag, I sat down and started typing and typing and typing. And I finished them. Kiddingly I stacked them neatly and went into the back area where I handed them to him and said, "Anything else, Boss?"

He couldn't believe what he was seeing. With a silly little giggle he said, "Yeah, do you want a job?"

"Sure. If it's part time."

"How's $50 a week?"

"Fine, if there's a raise every two months."

"How's tomorrow morning?"

"Eight?"

"Eight!"

And that's how that worked. I ended up doing the bookkeeping and letter writing and typed hardware schedules, while gradually learning the business and getting to know a super individual. He was a scrapper through and through. He had to be. At barely 5'4" and 110 pounds he had been a high school quarterback, and was Big Man on Campus.

Home life and hardware store life and acting life worked together to get me thinking of something bigger and better.

In 1950, disaster struck. After 23 years of hard work at General Motors, dad was let go. Except for an accident in 1930 he had never missed a day. A cost-cutting regime had come in, and 10 "gray heads," all department managers 50 years of age or older, were chopped. He was devastated. He wrote letters and resumes to various automotive companies. Nothing. He got in his car and visited General Motors Truck dealers he had helped over the years, one in Mobile, Alabama, and one in Ft. Worth. The car trip was planned really to get himself out of town, he told me years later. He was so embarrassed and hurt he couldn't face anyone.

The dealer in Ft. Worth needed money to survive so dad's pals at the plant made the Texan a deal he couldn't refuse. Take dad in as a partner or fold. So the family moved to Texas, leaving me alone in Birmingham.

I had enough money saved, about $2,000, so I decided to buy a new car, a 1950 Chevrolet. This would solve the transportation problem, until I had to drive in snow and ice. That winter, driving on Woodward Avenue one night coming out from Detroit, I saw the rain turn to snow, then to freezing rain. That was the first time I thought of living somewhere else. If I had to pick a moment, all these years later, when the first thought of a change crossed my mind, that was it. Bit by bit the pieces started falling in place. It was THINK BIG time again.

Looking back it was a matter of seeing what other people, older, more experienced and doing better than I, were doing, and had. And what they had wasn't good enough for me.

My brother Terry and his wife lived in nearby Jackson, Michigan, where he worked for Goodyear. Old house, no extra money, tight budget, solid future with the company, but never top management. Not for me.

The hardware store work was OK but I knew there was no future for me there. Russ's son Jack would be returning from Korea soon, and it was easy to see that "bookkeeper" and even "office manager" would be my title 20 years from then. I could see my work at WXYZ was limited too. The volume had not increased substantially since graduation. Livingston had cast me as Dan Reid, the Lone Ranger's nephew. I was doing all the kid's parts, exclusively, but it still was not enough. I was doing other radio shows, and an occasional TV show, but nothing that could point to a solid future.

Add all that up and you can understand that something better, somewhere, was beginning to build up in the back of my mind. Would it be a comfortable life in Birmingham, playing golf, running back and forth to Detroit, being comfortable around old family friends, or should I reach for the sky? The question that haunted me was where to reach.

My goals were now set: I wanted a full-time acting job. I wanted a new, beautiful home. I wanted to do all this in a warm climate.

Angel Voices heard me, and they began speaking.

First, my cousin Harry mentioned one day I ought to be thinking of New York or Hollywood and big network shows. In my own cocksure way I had an answer for him.

"I *am* doing big network shows. Three of them."

"I mean the really big network shows, like Lux Radio Theater, Jack Benny, Fibber McGee and Molly, Dragnet, I Love a Mystery. Big, big ones."

"But they're in Hollywood. I don't have the money to go all the way out there." And the discussion went on and on. He was right, but I couldn't see taking the risk. Still, he kept up the argument every time we were together. The seed was planted as to where the next step had to be.

About then another Angel Voice was heard from. A call for a cartoon voice-over at Jam Handy Studios came in. Two directors were in town from the Disney studios and had a job for me. It was a simple job, and we were finished in 15 minutes, which left ample time for me to sound them out about Hollywood.

"Say, by the way," I ventured cautiously, "if you ever hear of anything for me in Hollywood I wish you'd call me."

The older of the two wasted no time answering. "There's only one way to get started in Hollywood and that's to be there and work at it. Hollywood won't come to you."

"Yeah, but I don't have the money to take the gamble," I argued.

"Then save your money and when you're ready give it a shot. There's all kinds of competition out there. It won't happen overnight."

My want list was building, slowly but surely. Warmer weather, more acting work, better living conditions, more money. That eliminated New York and Chicago. It meant Hollywood. And once I nailed that down in my subconscious mind the Angels went to work.

The day after Thanksgiving, I had a 2:30 call for a Lone Ranger show. It was a gray, cold, blustery day, with snow flurries and occasional freezing rain. I was scared to death of driving on ice or in heavy snow but the show must go on, I said to myself, shivering. This day I got both ice and snow, plus cars spinning out of control all around me. With this in mind I took the widest, most heavily traveled roads to the studio, Woodward Avenue practically to the river, then East Jefferson to Iroquois. These were at least partially cleared. I guess I was complaining the minute I hit the studio door.

No one paid much attention to my complaining except, finally, Jack Petruzzi. During a break between rehearsals he jumped all over me. "If you don't like it here then go to

Hollywood where it's nice and warm," he said curtly. Jack knew. He had tried to make it "out there" but had come back broke . . . and broken. "But quit your lousy complaining. You're getting on my nerves."

I didn't say anything. Then as much to myself as anybody I said under my breath, "If I thought I had half a chance of making it, I'd do it."

"How old are you, 23, 24?" Jack snapped again.

"Twenty-four last March," I answered quietly, still deep in thought.

"Heck, what've you got to lose," he began his argument. "You're young, no family, no responsibilities, you've got a car and you've got what no other kid in Hollywood has."

"What's that," I asked, not being able to think of one thing.

"A college education, two years' training with the most experienced bunch of actors in the country and working for the toughest director anywhere," he went on, getting hotter by the second. "AND, to use you they don't have to put up with the lousy stage mothers or teachers or anything. If you don't like it here, then GO!" He got up angrily and left for the card game in the basement.

I hardly remember doing the show. Jack never said another word the rest of the day. I looked for him after the rebroadcast and he was gone. But the Angel had spoken its piece. And this time it stuck.

If there was just the slightest doubt in my mind whether the move to the west coast was right, it was resolved on my way home that night. While I was driving out Woodward Avenue, the snow turned to freezing rain and the street became an ice-skating rink. I held on for dear life, trying to keep the car straight. Then as if I wasn't even steering the car, it began a slow 360-degree turn, banged into a drift on the left side, bounced and did a 360 the other way. Fortunately for me there was no other traffic on either side. The cars in back slowed down and let me do my spins. Also, fortunately, the car ended up going straight down the highway in the same direction, toward Birmingham. *That* was it. There was no turning back.

My parents were all for it. They gave me the same "you're young so why not" assurances. I don't think they ever realized how enormous the gamble was.

In the end, and I've proven it for myself a dozen times since 1951, the decision is yours. The gamble is yours. When the thought first flashes into your mind, someone is trying to tell you something. I'm a firm believer in the old saying, "When a small door closes, a larger door has *already* opened." If you keep a positive attitude, then the right people at the right time will say the right things. Angel Voices. You can keep asking people what you should do until you are blue in the face. All you're doing is trying to find someone to agree with you. Actually, down deep, you know the answer. You can't appreciate this until you've thought it out, made the decision, then tried it.

The larger door was waiting for me. I had to take the gamble even if it cost me every dime I had to my name. I figured I had a month to get things in order. It seemed logical that I spend Christmas in Ft. Worth, then head out from there.

Telling Russ was the toughest part. I didn't find out until many years later he was really proud of me for making the decision. He had more guts and took more business gambles than anyone I have ever known. I guess he expected the same of me. He tried to help me the best he knew how. He knew the owner of an ad agency in Birmingham, who claimed to know important people in Hollywood. He asked him to give me letters of introduction. He also gave me a Christmas bonus, though '51 was not a good year for the business. Thank you, Russ, wherever you are.

January 5th, 1952, with many maps, three letters of introduction, a limited wardrobe, limited cash, and golf clubs, I headed out, before dawn.

12

The Knocking Pays Off

It was follow the sun. El Paso the first night, Yuma the second night, lunch in Indio the next day and by late afternoon I was in Hollywood. The next morning I called on the former assistant director at WXYZ, Ted Robertson, by now an assistant director at McCann-Erickson advertising agency. He got right to the cold hard facts.

"There's only one way and it will be tough," advised Ted. "Go up to the eighth floor and check in with AFRA. They'll give you a list of all radio shows in town. Be on the street at 8 a.m. and knock on doors and keep knocking on doors. Try to get past the secretaries and audition for the directors. At least sign in on their Actors Call List. Make out 3x5 cards, with full particulars and your credits. For you this is tough because you don't have any credits out here yet. But believe me, when you tell them that you worked in Detroit, most directors will at least give you a listen. Chuck Livingston was murder to work for, how well I know."

So my 8-to-5 knocking began. Five days a week. When the alarm clock went off, the shock waves set in. I learned the first day on the street my work consisted of knocking on doors and trying desperately to get past the secretaries, who were bound and determined not to let me disturb the directors, who hired the actors.

"I'm sorry, Mr. Beals," and she said it as if she really wasn't, "but Mr. Smith just isn't auditioning new actors today. But if you will come back, say about June, he might be able to see you for a few moments."

The three letters of introduction that I had counted on so heavily were a disappointment. The executive at a large radio station, which turned out to be KMPC, hardly remembered the ad executive in Birmingham. To boot, he had nothing to do with actors. He was "only the bookkeeper." I couldn't locate the announcer/actor in the phone book. So I checked with Ted Robertson. He told me that he hadn't been working much here and had headed to New York for greener pastures. Letter No. 3 was worse. The director had died three years before.

I knew the weather in January would be unlike that in Michigan. At least no snow. But two days after I arrived on January 7 it started to rain. Five days later after much flooding, the sun finally reappeared.

Fortunately, the deluge worked to my advantage. I was the

only actor on the street making calls. Some of the directors I had to see were actually in their offices. I actually got to read for some of them. But an on-the-air job was what I needed. Quite by accident it almost happened a few days after I arrived during one of many cloudbursts, as we called them in Michigan.

Someone with the Lone Ranger cast had given me the name of Hugh Studebaker. Hugh was the "father" on the Beulah Show and a veteran actor.

I called his residence and was told he was working at Western Recorders on Sunset. Flood or no flood, I was off like a shot. To get to see a fellow actor and maybe a director at the same time was too exciting a prospect to pass by.

The receptionist directed me to the studio. I quietly opened the door to the control room and edged my way in. It was quite empty, but I could see the cast milling around in the studio waiting for the first read-through to begin. I decided which one was Hugh Studebaker and made my move.

Out the door of the control room I zoomed, and acting as if I owned the place I entered the studio and approached my man like a long lost friend. He didn't know what was happening.

"Hugh, my name is Dick Beals from Detroit. All the guys on the Ranger show wanted me to say hello to you the minute I got to town. Can we chat a minute?"

"Why, I guess so," the dapper, gray-haired professional said hesitantly. "Let's go up to the clients booth." Out of the corner of my eye I could see him shrugging his shoulders at the cast as he led the way.

"We have plenty of time," he said directing me to a chair in the plush room. "They can't find the kid that plays my son. The director is about nuts. They've about had it with him."

"What's his name?"

"Stuffy Singer and he's a . . . pill," winced Studebaker, trying to say something nice.

"Too bad he didn't work for a guy like Charles D. Livingston, huh?" I said, with a big grin.

He just nodded and shook his head. I could tell he was trying to listen to me and keep an eye on the studio below so I made it quick and reviewed my background and plan of attack.

"Any chance I could meet your director and make an appointment to read for him, Mr. Studebaker?" I asked.

"Well, we can try. Stuffy is the only kid on the show, but you never know. But now is not the time to talk to this director." Then he paused, trying to conjure up something the least bit positive. "Tell you what. If you have time why not stay right here? You can listen to the rehearsal and if I see a good time to do the honors, I'll give you the high sign and we'll try it. How does that sound?''

Thinking of the monsoon awaiting me outside, his plan sounded great and I told him so. Down he went and I could see him join the other cast members. All of them had disgusted looks and were constantly checking watches. Then the director came storming in and said, ''To heck with him . . . let's start reading.'' He jerked back his chair at the head of the conference table, upsetting it with a bang.

Hugh sidled over cautiously and getting the director's attention, talked quietly into his ear with his back to the table so no one could hear him. The director didn't move. Hugh kept talking, pointing up at me with his eyes. The director thought for about five seconds and nodded OK. With that, Hugh stepped back and motioned me to ''get down here quicker than quick.''

I burst into that studio and was at his side like that.

''Dick, this is Mr. Pettit, our director.''

Shaking my hand Pettit said, ''This is highly unusual but if you could read Billy's part until the other actor gets here, it would really help us.''

''Certainly, I'd love to,'' I said, trying to hide my absolute delight.

Motioning to his secretary he said, ''Give Mr. Beals a script and let's get going.''

''Play him about eight, nine, ten?'' I asked, trying to let him know I could play it any way he wanted.

''Ten's OK. Everybody, this is Dick Beals. He's just out from Detroit where he's been doing all of their radio shows. Please introduce yourselves later. Let's do it; we're way behind.''

While they began, I marked my script in a hurry. What a thrill. Actually working with these famous Hollywood voices. I was actually working in Hollywood.

The lines told me he was a flippant but bright kid, so I played him that way.

Hugh kept looking down at me (he made sure he sat right next to me, which I appreciated) and nodded or wrote little notes of recommendations or whatever. It seemed like seconds for the 15-minute show to be over.

''OK, let's be ready on mike in five minutes. Mr. Beals, very nice. Please stay with us just in case,'' said Pettit, looking back from his half trot to the control room.

Hugh introduced me all around, names I had heard for years.

''Sit tight,'' he whispered in my ear, ''You just might have walked into something big.''

Sit tight I did. For four minutes and 30 seconds I sat tight. Then just as Pettit hit the talk-back button to get us up for the production rehearsal, 10-year-old Stuffy Singer sauntered in. The director, like a shot, came flying into the studio.

He sat him down at the conference table and pulled up the chair next to him. He was hot. "You're late, Stuff. You've held up the whole cast. If you don't want to be on this radio show, we can arrange it. Do you understand what I'm saying?"

Stuff wasn't talking.

By this time Mrs. Singer had hurried into the studio and caught just the end of the conversation . . . the loss of income part.

The heated discussion went on. Apologies from the stage mother. Threats by the director, his threats culminating by his pointing at me saying, "We have someone here who could replace you *right now* if that's the way you want it." Then pounding his finger on the table with each word he said, "The next time you are late for a rehearsal, this man has your part. Is that clear, Stuff?"

Stuff nodded, head bowed. His mother jumped inside out, agreeing to everything in her fright.

"Hugh and Mr. Beals, would you join me in the control room?" Pettit asked. "Get your script marked, Stuff, and hurry up!"

He led the way in and when we were all there he paused long enough to collect himself. Running his fingers through his thinning hair, he then said to me, "I appreciate what you did, Mr. Beals, and I meant what I said out there. One slip on his part and we'll be calling you." With that he motioned to his secretary and continued, "We'll pay you for the rehearsal time. It won't be much, but maybe there will be more in the future." With that he shook my hand and hurried back to the studio.

Hugh shook my hand, winked and whispered, "Great job. The cast is all for you." With that he left hurriedly. After filling out the W-4 I headed back to the monsoon, suddenly realizing I had failed to put on my raincoat.

As I sloshed my way back to the car, my mind was going a mile a minute, trying to sort things out. What a confidence builder. I always knew I could compete out here or anywhere for that matter. If I worked at it hard, like at 110%, the work just had to be there. And that was my plan. THINK BIG. All my life those two words had paid off for me. Now I really wanted them to pay off . . . and soon.

The next morning the alarm announced another sunny day, so up and at 'em. Although it started out just like the rest, the confidence builder from the day before quickened my step. My meditation that morning centered upon the thought, "Divine Love supplies my needs and prospers my ways." I figured with

God at my side, everything would be in perfect order.

First call was in the Lawyers Building just off Vine and a block north of Sunset. The name was Wade Advertising, the director was Forrest Owen, and the shows were One Man's Family and the Curt Massey and Martha Tilton Show, sponsored by Miles Labs. Just to see those names in print gave me goose bumps. Another actor had given me their name, when he noticed it wasn't on my AFRA list. He warned me that the cast of One Man's Family was set and the Curt Massey show didn't use actors, but my rule was to call on every name in town, so Mr. Owen was going to get a call, come hell or high water. The high water I had survived.

The secretary, professional looking and nicely dressed, listened to my appeal patiently.

"Hi, I'd like to see Mr. Owen, please, and give him this card," I said, flashing my rather empty 3x5 resume.

Knowing what I was going to say, she was prepared instantly with her answer.

"I'm sorry, sir, but Mr. Owen is not seeing people today. This is 'show day.' His schedule is really busy."

"Certainly, I can understand how busy he is," I pleaded, "but it's really important that I get to see him. How about tomorrow?"

"No, I'm sorry, but let's see . . . ." And with that she started leafing through her calendar. "How about, in say, six weeks."

I hauled out my date book and counted off six very empty pages.

Before I could say anything she jumped in with . . . "Well, now let's see. How about Wednesday, March 16? Would that be convenient?"

"Nine o'clock?" I suggested, as I looked up from my busy notetaking. I knew that would be my 25th birthday and I wouldn't know anyone to celebrate with anyway.

"Nine would be fine, Mr . . . ?" She hesitated, pencil poised.

"Beals. Dick Beals, B-e-a-l-s," I replied.

"Mr. Beals for Mr. Owen on the 16th of March," she wrote. "Please give us a call, say on the 14th, just to confirm, will you?" she said, smiling.

"Of course," I replied, trying to hide my frustration. "See you on the 16th." And off I went to my next appointment with my next door.

I learned early on that actors congregated in the back halls outside the studios at NBC. This meant that I had to work my way past the guard just inside the door at the Actors' Entrance just off Vine. Next I learned that the magic words were, "I'm auditioning in B this morning," and in I went.

Against the wall just outside the announcer's lounge was a machine that performers grew to know and love. I don't remember what this contraption was called but the actors answering service, RATE, an acronym for Radio Actors Telephone Exchange, could write your name on it in their offices just down the street; and in a scrawling handwritten style, a pen would write your name on the roll of paper and you could call and see who wanted you.

I used this time to visit with and get to know other actors. They were handy providers of names and shows and people to see. If I needed a good word or a recommendation or information about a new show that was auditioning people, these folks were just super. They were anxious for me to make it, and their encouragement every day was just what the doctor ordered.

But this was the day that things were going to click. "Divine Love supplies my needs and prospers my ways." My first call had gotten me the usual brush-off so I mentally wrote that off. While my fellow actors were all sitting on the green leather couches asking me about my classmate back at Michigan State, the Olympic, now pro boxer Chuck Davey, someone in back of me watching the contraption scratch away said, "Hey Dick, RATE wants you."

I couldn't believe it. I hustled over and sure enough there was my name scrawled clumsily by the big awkward pen. Could this possibly be my first call? Trying not to act nervous or anxious and not fooling anyone, I ran to the phone booth and dialed with an inspired index finger.

"RATE, Alice," said the friendly voice.

"Alice, this is Dick Beals. You're looking for me?" (Oh please, dear God, someone be looking for me.)

"Yes, Dick, call Ted Robertson at McCann-Erickson regarding a Dr. Christian Show. Do you have the number?"

"Yes, thank you. I'll call them right away."

I found the number and called McCann. I got the secretary, and trying to sound calm, I asked for Mr. Robertson.

"I'm sorry, Mr. Beals, but Mr. Robertson just stepped out," she responded.

I visibly slumped. I didn't know what to say. As it turned out I didn't have to say anything. The secretary was reading me like a book.

"Thanks for getting back to us so quickly. We have a Dr. Christian call for you. Do you have a pencil and paper?" she asked mechanically.

The magic words in this business—"call." Paper and pen flew up against the wall. "Yes, I do, go ahead."

"The call is for 2 p.m., Wednesday, January 27, at CBS, studio B. It is for a six-year-old boy. Neil Reagan will direct. Are you available?"

"Yes, ma'am," I choked. "I'm confirming, and thank you."

The doors rattled darned near off the hinges as I broke back for the group still sitting on the couch. They were all smiles. Actor Jan Arvan had the biggest grin.

"Going to do Dr. Christian next week, huh?" The rest of them were grinning from ear to ear.

"How did you know?" I squeaked.

"Ted told me yesterday," said Jan. "Nice going. Congratulations and all that stuff."

Now all the others were up shaking my hand, while I was trying to hide the tears. Was I thrilled! I was actually going to work with Jean Hersholt and Rosemary DeCamp, on a live network radio show before a live audience.

"Come on," said Bill Justine, "let's go across the street and buy the kid a cup of coffee before he collapses."

Over coffee I asked Jan why he hadn't told me I was going to get the call.

"An important lesson to be learned about this town," began the old hand, choosing his words carefully. "You never have a job until you are there in the studio with a script with your name on it in your hand." Bill Justine took it from there.

"I got a job in a picture . . . needed the money real bad. I had the script and the call. Then made the mistake of telling another actor my good news." Bill sipped his coffee, studied his cup for a moment and went on.

"My 'friend' swore under his breath saying . . . 'that guy promised me a part in that picture.' The next day I got a call from the director's office informing me he had decided to use someone else." Long pause. Dead silence at the table. Then without looking up, Bill said, "Guess who got the part?"

"The real pros don't do things like that, Dick," said Jan. "But keep things to yourself until you are in the studio."

The coffee celebration ended. I continued my calls until I just plain ran out of gas and headed home to my hotel. As I walked through the lobby, another event occurred that was to play a big part in my career. An elderly woman resident stopped me as I was heading for the dining room. She had a leather wallet on her lap.

"Son," she said, trying to catch my attention. "Here is that wallet I promised you. I made it myself. Do you still want it?"

Truly I had forgotten about it. I didn't really need one, and I don't think I ever said I would buy it, but . . . it was a day for celebrating.

"It's only $1," she pleaded. "I carved the leather myself. It has nice plastic card holders in it."

"Sure I want it," I lied as I exchanged the dollar bill for the wallet. I thanked her, complimented her on her workmanship, put the wallet in my back pocket and headed for dinner.

Later that evening I got out the thing and began cleaning out my old wallet. In the last plastic holder I pulled out the contents, and to my surprise out floated a little piece of paper. I unfolded it and read in total disbelief.

At the top left corner . . . From the Desk of:

Jack McCarthy

Station Manager WXYZ

In Jack's handwriting: "See Forrest Owen at Wade Advertising."

With all the confusion and excitement of coming to Hollywood, I had forgotten all about this. Jack McCarthy not only was the station manager at WXYZ, he was the voice of the Green Hornet. I remember his coming up to me one night after a show and asking about the news that I was going to take a shot at Hollywood. He knew what I was up against.

After I had finished telling him my plans, he asked me to wait a minute. He ducked into his office and came back with this slip of paper that I was now reading two months and 1,900 miles later.

"Forey used to work here as an announcer," said Jack in his famous Green Hornet voice. "I don't know what he's doing now, but at least drop in and say hello for me."

Oh Jack, will I! Needless to say, my March 16, 9 a.m. appointment had just been moved up to 9 a.m. the very next morning. I couldn't wait.

At 8:59 the next morning, the very same secretary looked at me kind of funny as I strode up to her desk. With the most serious look I could muster and without saying word one, I took out the note. No hello, no nothing. I had planned it very carefully.

With a dramatic flair I put the note barely six inches from her nose and said, "Dick Beals to see Mr. Owen. Jack McCarthy sent me, and don't mess around with the Green Hornet." And I just froze. The note never budged a fraction of an inch.

Neither did she at first. Then she very carefully reached up, took the note, got up slowly as if I had a gun pointed at her, backed away from her desk and opened a door that appeared to go down a hallway.

I held on for dear life. After about 15 long seconds she returned. She slowly sat back down at her desk, handed me my note and said calmly, "Mr. Owen will see you now. It's the last door on the left.''

I zipped around her desk and headed down the hall, afraid to look back. His door was open, so I knocked on the frame, and the real live Forrest Owen was already making his way around his desk with his hand out. He wasn't more than 5'10'', but solid, athletic-looking, with a friendly, warm smile.

"So the Green Hornet sent you, did he?" he chuckled and indicated I should sit down in one of two chairs. "How is old Jack?" "I saw him just before Christmas," I replied, trying desperately not to show how uncomfortable I was. "He seemed OK, but I didn't know him except to do the Hornet show."

He moved quickly around to his desk chair. His desk was well organized with stacks of scripts in their assigned spots. His title was Radio & Television Director, and I got the impression he was all business.

"How long had you been working in Detroit and what kind of work were you doing?" He seemed genuinely interested.

"I started in the fall of '48 while I was a senior at Michigan State, doing a live television series for the J. L. Hudson Company," I began. I thought there was just the slightest reaction in his eyes. "That led to a radio show by the same agency; the star of that show told the director at WXYZ about me, and he gave me a shot doing a Quaker Oats commercial on Challenge of the Yukon. Sort of an on-the-air audition. The head director, Mr. Livingston . . . ''

"Charles D. Livingston," mused Mr. Owen, shaking his head in disbelief. "What a wild man. How did you two get along?"

"He scared me half to death but he kept calling me. I did all their shows for three years. Whenever a kid's voice came up he cast me. I did all ages from babies to 14 and 15-year-olds."

"So you went to Michigan State? That's my alma mater. Class of '41," he grinned. "Were you a radio major too?"

"Yes, class of '49. They did an outstanding job of preparing me for this profession. I'll be forever grateful. If it hadn't been for Dr. Robert Coleman at WKAR, I never would have gotten into this end of the business. I went there intending to be the world's greatest sports announcer. He pointed me in the right direction real quick."

"Yes, Bob Coleman helped a lot of us get pointed in the right direction," he said, gazing off somewhere over my head. "I was an announcer of sorts there and then went off to WXYZ after graduation. Did Jack tell you that I was on his announcer staff for a while?"

I nodded in the affirmative. "Yes, and I got the idea he'd like to hear from you. He was not quite sure what you were doing now."

76

He nodded, as if making a mental note. "Well, let's talk about you. How are things going?" he asked, again with that genuine interest, but quickly glancing at his watch.

"Well, I'm knocking on doors trying to get directors to listen to me." I sighed. "I'm doing Dr. Christian next week. Making headway. It's slow going."

He leaned back, scratching his head, as though planning his next words carefully. "It's too bad you weren't here in November or December. We just finished auditioning over 600 people from coast to coast for a voice for a new character called Speedy Alka-Seltzer." Pointing to an artist's rendering on the couch behind me he said, "That's Speedy. We plan to have him be the spokesman for our client Miles Laboratories on TV and radio." He jumped up, came around his desk, got the drawing and propped it up on the chair next to me. Leaning against the corner of his desk, he continued . . .

"This will be a huge project. All stop-motion animation, using a Speedy doll about 4" high. First of its kind."

As I looked at the drawing, that same freon gas feeling swept through me. Just for a flash. An Angel Voice? I wasn't sure, but I shivered from head to toe. Alka-Seltzer was one of the biggest advertisers in America. Back behind his desk he paused, waiting for me to say something. I didn't know what to say.

"Well," he broke the silence, "as I said, the auditions were closed last month. Sorry you weren't here. But . . . maybe something else will come up. If it does I'll give you a shot at it. And if you are around CBS some afternoon, drop into the Massey-Tilton show." He got up from behind his desk, an invitation for me to leave.

He gave a friendly handshake. I thanked him and headed back down the hallway not knowing whether or not I wanted to see the secretary again that day. She was still there. As I passed her desk heading toward the door I said, "Thank you, hope to see you again."

She responded pleasantly, "Hope so, too. Good luck."

I didn't believe in luck then and still don't. "Luck Is When Preparation Meets Opportunity." Or as coach John McKay once said, "Luck takes over after you have given 110%." With those words in mind, I reached for my call list and had at it.

13

Speedy is Born

Time passed quickly. Nervous time set in as my Dr. Christian day neared. Well, not really nervous time. I guess apprehensive would be a better word.

Naturally, I arrived at CBS 45 minutes early. The quiet, empty, darkened studio didn't help the waiting. The engineer arrived. Ted and his secretary arrived. Scripts were distributed around the large conference table. Lights came on, letting me see the size of the place for the first time. It looked like a small theater. It seated about 300 and had a raised stage; curtains covered all the walls, and there was a mike set up near the footlights with another mike on a table on the far side, where I guessed Jean Hersholt would sit. And to my absolute amazement, there was a mike, at a height of about four feet, next to the cast mike. It was mine.

The cast started to arrive, along with Mr. Hersholt and Rosemary DeCamp. Everyone knew one another. I was the outsider and Ted introduced me as quickly as he could. When Neil Reagan, Ronald Reagan's older brother, came in, the socializing ceased and we got to work.

The time went quickly. Out here they did things a bit differently from Detroit. They had a relaxed read-through around a conference table. As we went along, the characters were described by Reagan, with actors slowly working into the parts. My part was short but it gave me a chance to emote. This kid went from scared to crying to terrified. I gave it all I had in the first read-through, which was the way I had been trained. Out here it wasn't expected.

Mr. Reagan looked over his glasses and said smiling, ''I hope you're saving something for the show, Mr. Beals. You have three more rehearsals to go, you know.''

I shrugged, looked embarrassed and fidgeted. ''I'm fine. I wanted you to hear it the way I thought it should be done.''

We went on. I glanced at Ted and shrugged my shoulders. He grinned and gave me a big wink. So did the actress next to him named Ginny Gregg, the actor next to her named Hal March, and the actor next to him named Whitfield Conner. I recognized the voices but this was the first time I knew their names. The rest of the cast had familiar voices but again I didn't know any names.

What Ted Robertson had done, bless his heart, was to cast the biggest names in Hollywood for this particular show. Everyone at that table, except me, did every radio show in town. They were legends. He did it for me. He wanted these people to spread the word. Now *that's* class. I found out later, many times, that they did spread the word. It started me off with a bang.

During the breaks everyone made it a point to introduce himself and just the mention of Detroit and WXYZ raised eyebrows. It was the only training I had had, but it was the perfect place to have started, I was now learning.

Working before a live audience wasn't new. We did that every week at Michigan State. And live network wasn't new; we did that in Detroit. But live network *and* a live audience was new.

They did something else that surprised me but gave me a huge thrill. The announcer introduced the cast to the audience before airtime. Art Gilmore was thoughtful enough to mention prior to my entrance I was doing my first show in Hollywood. The audience applauded loudly. I found myself smiling through watery eyes.

I got edgy as the second hand on the studio clock headed toward airtime and Neil Reagan said, "Stand by." Once the red light went on it was all business and all concentration.

Everything went great. I loved it. When I did my crying scene I got caught up in it and left the mike wiping my eyes with a Kleenex.

As I sat down where the cast sat I noticed Ted in the control room holding up a note against the glass. Slowly I wandered over and the note read, "YOU HAM." I just shrugged my shoulders, saying silently, "Talent will out."

Announcer Art Gilmore ended the show, and the second we were off the air, he giggled and said to the audience, "Isn't that a silly way to make a living." The audience applauded and laughed. It was over.

The cast was most kind, all saying "Good luck" and "See you next time." Neil Reagan was most complimentary. Ted was proud of his handiwork. What a day.

The magic continued. I figured out a better way to see directors. I sat outside the director's booth waiting until he was finished with his show. Talking quickly I explained what I did, especially mentioning Detroit and the Ranger and Hornet and now Dr. Christian, and gave him my 3x5 card. In time I had all their schedules down on a list and was always there when they exited.

I started getting the calls. Tarzan, Wild Bill Hickok, Richard Diamond with Dick Powell (thanks to Ginny Gregg). Ginny turned out to be the most helpful person I knew.

February 5 really proved to be a magic day. When I got back to the hotel a message to call Forrest Owen was waiting for me. I called his office immediately.

"Dick, I just had a thought, and don't feel you have to do it," he began, sounding more tired than I felt. "Tonight I'm going to be at Radio Recorders doing some Alka-Seltzer commercials with the One Man's Family cast. If you'd like to, drop in around 7:15 or so—you could try some of that Speedy Alka-Seltzer copy."

Now the auditions were closed I didn't see much sense to it, but it would give me a chance to read for him anyway. Miles and Alka-Seltzer just happened to be the No. 2 sponsor in the country for radio and No. 3 for television.

"That would be great, Mr. Owen," I said quickly. "I'll be there and thanks for thinking of me."

As usual I was early. He hadn't mentioned a studio number, but I heard general hubbub behind the big doors with Studio A on them so I opened the door and saw Ginny Gregg; knowing she was a regular on One Man's Family, I figured this must be the place. She waved me in. Then I saw Mr. Owen in the control room and he saw me. He talked briefly to the engineer, who quickly looked at me and headed out to set up a mike.

Mr. Owen pressed the talk-back switch, told the group they could take a 10-minute break, and added, "Dick Beals is here and we want to record something."

As they left, Mr. Owen came in with a couple of scripts. Handing them to me he said, "You determine the voice. But we're looking for an articulate, ageless voice, an enthusiastic character. Here is the song. I don't have a lead sheet but the tune is 'Alouette.' Let us know when you're ready."

While he was walking back to the control room and he and the engineer were getting set, I ran over it as quickly as I could. I figured for the first go-around I would play it straight, in my natural voice, no gimmicks, with as much energy as possible, and with a lot of sell and a big smile.

"Give us a level, please," said the tough-looking engineer, before I was really ready. I read the first few lines and sang a few bars of the song, as the engineer balanced the volume. "OK," he said, nodding at me through the glass.

Mr. Owen asked, "Are you ready?" I nodded yes. He slated, "Dick Beals as Speedy, take one," and pointed to me.

I just did it. It was "me." Nothing tricky, just as straight and clean as I could make it. I couldn't have asked for a clearer voice that night.

At the conclusion I looked up. Mr. Owen was talking to the engineer, who nodded, and then he pushed the talk-back.

"OK, thank you very much for coming in, Dick."

"Mr. Owen," I pleaded, "I have some other things I'd like to try."

"No, that's just fine, thanks for coming in," he said and gave a short wave, a quick smile and turned back to the engineer.

End of audition. I waved back and headed for the car. Dejected? Well, disappointed is probably a better word. Auditions are auditions, but in this particular case a job as national TV and radio spokesman for a major corporation was the dream of a lifetime. I dreaded thinking that if I had just tried something a bit different, a little bit better . . . ! Oh well, life must go on.

And it did. I really forgot all about that day. Calls were coming in with regularity. I was a working actor in Hollywood. I even had conflicts. Sometimes I worked so hard to get a certain director to use me and then suddenly he did . . . and I already had another call for the same time. I was tempted to suddenly become ill and cancel the first one. But the pros told me early on never to do that. Directors talk. But, oh how it hurt to turn down a call!

Ginny Gregg was one of my biggest boosters, and quite by accident, she played a major role in helping me get work, a lot of work. It happened on a day when a bunch of us were sitting around in the lobby of CBS.

"Hey busy actor," she said, grinning at me. "Which of the directors upstairs here have you met?"

"Well, none, actually," I said. "I got to see Mr. Del Valle's secretary, but she told me not to bother seeing the directors at CBS."

"Why not?" Ginny cried in disbelief.

"She said Mr. Del Valle's wife does all the kid's parts and I wouldn't stand a chance."

"She said WHAT?" Her eyes flashed all sorts of colors. "You come with me." With that she grabbed my wrist and hauled me to the elevator. When the door opened, she yanked me in and smashed the button for floor three and tapped her foot as the elevator slowly responded. It opened and down the aisle we went. She dragged me past the first secretary into the first director's office as a startled Elliott Lewis looked up.

"Elliott, from this moment on, never use me for kid's parts, on Suspense or any of the other shows you direct. Use Dick Beals. Is that clear? He's better than I will ever be."

And without waiting for an answer, down the aisle we went to the next office and the next one and the next one. Same story. Same startled director. When we got to the last office there sat Mr. Del Valle's secretary. Ginny, followed by my wrist and then me, flew into Mr. Del Valle's office. The man behind

81

the desk, tanned, steel-gray hair, crew cut, ex-marine type, continued reading the script on his desk. He slowly raised his arm and waved a hello.

"Jaime, listen to me for a second," she began impatiently. "This is Dick Beals. He does kid's voices. Use him. Don't use me ever again." Silence. Long pause. "Are you listening, Jaime?"

He never looked up. "OK, dear, anything you say," he murmured. "Be talking to you soon, Dick." Silence. Longer pause. "What are we having for dinner, honey? I'll be home right after the show . . . 'bout 6:30."

Mission accomplished. In less than five minutes I was locked in to every CBS radio show. Shows like Suspense, Lineup, Gunsmoke, Have Gun Will Travel, Amos and Andy and Edgar Bergen and Charlie McCarthy. The last CBS radio show . . . Gunsmoke . . . went off the air six years later. God bless you, Virginia Gregg, wherever you are.

As weeks went by, the calls were more and more frequent. In fact, I was tabbed the busiest actor in town. Despite the work, which for an actor is never enough, I continued making calls eight to five, five days a week. Then I was to get a call that changed my whole life.

"Dick, this is Forrest Owen," said that warm, friendly, all-business voice. "I just wanted you to know that Miles Laboratories has made a decision on the voice of Speedy Alka-Seltzer. It's YOU!"

Silence. I couldn't talk. I didn't know what to say. Nothing like this had ever happened to me before. The magnitude of the whole thing floored me.

"Are you there?" he asked. "Did you hear me?"

"Yes, I'm, uh, yes," I gasped. "I just can't believe, uh . . . I wanted it so much and I had just kind of . . . well . . . I thought it went to somebody else, since it took so long."

"These things take time," he said patiently. "There were over 600 people out there wanting to be Speedy." And then the all-business voice took over again. "What this means is this. We propose to offer you a contract. The contract will say that you agree to perform as Speedy if and when the market testing is satisfactory. Is that OK with you?"

What could I say? I was just 25. I wouldn't know a contract if I saw one. I just wanted to work and get paid. But I felt I could trust Mr. Forrest Owen. "Sounds fine. When do we get started?" I asked hesitantly.

"How about coming in tomorrow morning about 10; we'll go over the contract, and I'll fill you in on what's ahead."

"Ten is fine. I'll be there. And thank you," I said.

He chuckled, slightly. Then in the nicest, friendliest voice I had ever heard, he said, "Congratulations . . . Speedy."

The meeting with Mr. Owen the next morning was again all business. "The plan is this. Scripts probably will be ready and approved by August or September."

"Why does it take so long? That's three months."

"Because it does." His jaw tightened just a bit. "First we have to do our marketing homework, create the spots to fit the marketing goals and objectives, then go through the approval process. Here is the contract. You are agreeing to do the voice of Speedy in these upcoming test spots and agreeing to be put under an exclusive contract as the voice of Speedy if Miles Laboratories decides to continue with the project." He handed me the contract, which consisted of several pages. I started reading it.

"I'd rather you take it home and read it carefully. If you want to have an attorney go over it, fine," he stated in that firm way he had of saying things.

"No. I'd rather just read it here for a minute and ask questions if that is all right."

"OK, let me leave you alone for a minute, then," he said as he got up and headed for the door. "Make yourself comfortable."

I didn't really know what I was looking for, not ever having seen a contract before. But what he said was right there in plain English. The only protection for their client was that I was agreeing not to do a similar voice for a competitive product. I guess some people might think of doing that, but I just wasn't brought up that way. We were taught honesty from day one.

As he walked back in I questioned that last point. "Define this exclusivity point so we are all saying the same thing," I said. "Just what do you consider a competitive product to be?"

"OK." He chose his next words carefully. "A competitive product is any other headache or stomach remedy type product."

"What if, uh, say, Anacin wanted me to do a little kid's voice on a commercial? Could I do it?" I asked.

He grabbed his forehead and leaned back in his chair. "No, that's playing it too close," he said as he rocked back forward. "This contract isn't meant to keep you from working. But our client wants the Speedy voice protected. So use your own judgment."

Where I got this next line I'll never know, but I'm glad I did. "Let's do it this way then. If I have any doubt I'll call you and get your OK."

"That's more than fair," he answered quickly.

"Where do I sign then?" I asked.

I signed my very first contract; he signed it and we shook

hands. He didn't show any emotion, but I sensed he was as pleased about this whole thing as I was. Pleased? I was so excited my insides were jumping all over the place.

As I was leaving he said, "Sometime this week drop on over to CBS around four o'clock or so and visit the Massey-Tilton show. I'd like you to meet everybody." That remark topped my whole day even more. It made me feel a part of a team, an important part. With my sports background, that meant a great deal to me.

Driving home to my hotel I didn't know what to feel or think. The contract in my pocket was a milestone in my fledgling career. But contract or no contract, being Speedy wasn't bringing in any money, so it was not time to slow down and celebrate. It was time to get back to knocking on doors and meeting directors outside their studios. "Divine Love supplies my needs and prospers my ways."

ow a senior at Michigan State, the ring of 1949 finds Dick at WXYZ dio, Detroit, rehearsing for a Lone anger show. This is obviously a osed picture. Dick didn't have the xury of his own microphone in etroit.

Below right) January 1952, ollywood, Dick performs on his first ollywood radio show, Dr. Christian.

few weeks later, Dick performs on e Wild Bill Hickok radio show, with tars Guy Madison and Andy Devine. his is a posed picture, for a magazine rticle. In Hollywood, Dick was rovided with his own microphone.

14

Dick Meets the Stars

One show on my list was underlined in heavy pencil . . . The Jack Benny Show. It was a must. The roadblock was the casting director, Hilliard Marx, Mary Livingston's brother. He was tough to see . . . almost impossible. I had made call after call and his secretary just wouldn't budge. But one rainy day the odds changed.

His name was on my call list that day, and finding myself on the corner of Hollywood Boulevard and Vine and slightly damp, I once again took three deep breaths and charged into his office. For the first time, his secretary wasn't at her desk. Seeing his office door open and the man himself sitting there with his nose deep in scripts, I knocked on the door frame.

"Mr. Marx, my name is Dick Beals. Could I talk to you for a minute?" I was kind of moving on in slowly.

"I really don't have time," he mumbled, ignoring me completely. "What do you want?" Long pause . . . nose still in the script. "What are you doing out of school?"

Hilliard Marx had Coke bottle bottoms for glasses. I mean thick. He never did look up to see who was in his office. I didn't quite know how to play this one. Go first-class, I figured. THINK BIG.

"I'm not in school anymore, Mr. Marx, I graduated several years ago." I said politely.

"Did, huh?" he muttered, still buried.

"Yes, sir. I'm a new actor in town. I do kids' voices. I'd like to audition for your show. Could I read something for you today?"

Still no look.

"I can do kids' voices from infants through 14 or 15, boys' and girls' voices, animal voices . . . ."

"You have a good voice, kid. Nice and clear. But we don't use many kids on the show." At this, and for the first time interested in my presence, he looked me over carefully, and going back to his script, he said, "Have your mother leave your name and address with my secretary and if anything comes up, I'll give you a call." Then he slowly looked up again and said, "Graduated? From what?" and his eyes refocused on the scripts.

I was ticked and couldn't hold back the anger. Slapping both sweaty palms on his shiny glass-topped desk, I said, "I graduated from Michigan State! Class of '49! And my parents live in Texas! I live alone here!"

His next move couldn't have been duplicated by the best actor in town. He froze, as if his mind had just caught up with him. He slowly looked up at me and focused as best he could. I just stared at him, all business, with just the slightest smile.

Now he was embarrassed but didn't want to show it. So he fidgeted and squirmed and cleared his throat, and the stammering began. "Well, you see, uh, well, we never allow adults to do kids' voices on our show." He cleared his throat noisily again. "We use kids exclusively. We have a live audience and we wouldn't dare try to fool them. You can understand that."

Go first-class, I thought. Why not? "It's your show, Mr. Marx. But on this card I'm going to leave with you regardless of your policy, please note that I regularly do The Railroad Hour, Fibber McGee and Molly, Dr. Christian, Lux Radio Theater . . . all shows before a live audience. The directors aren't trying to fool anyone." With my two cents still echoing around his office, I reached across to hand him my card, shook his limp hand, thanked him for his time and left. My last fit of temper was taken out on his office door, which was properly slammed shut, but not before locking it from the inside. Let him explain *that* to his secretary.

The Jack Benny Show was the only Hollywood radio show that actually had parts for me to do that I never did. Mr. Marx was a hard loser.

Of all the shows I did, The Railroad Hour was a big favorite. It starred Gordon McCrae, with Carmen Dragon and the NBC Orchestra. The live music was superb and his guest artists were the biggest names in the music business. One guest artist, Margaret Truman, almost did me in.

We always had a read-through Sunday evening at 7 p.m. By the time I got there most of the cast was there; and spotting an empty chair, I headed for it as the secretary handed me my script. I had a habit of scanning the title sheet just to see who the guest star was. I forget the title but I read, "Starring Gordon McCrae with his guest star Miss Margaret Truman . . . ." At that spot I guess my eyes lit up. I was about to say, being a devout Republican, "Look who we're going to have to put up with . . . ."

But Gordon must have been reading my mind. He quickly said, "Dick, I don't think you've met Miss Truman."

The person sitting at my right elbow said demurely, "Good evening, Mr. Beals, I'm Margaret Truman," as she reached to shake my hand.

Thank you, Gordon, wherever you are.

Lux Radio Theater gave me another chance to be less than professional. The show was The Third Man. I forget who the stars were but they were not the original cast. I think Ray Milland played the Joseph Cotten part. My part was a little German boy, who spoke fluent German, of course. I didn't. To help the cast, the director brought in some professors from USC to play background parts and assist us non-German-speaking types.

My big line was, "Er geht in den Keller." By airtime I was as good as I was going to be. During rehearsals, my tutors had moaned and groaned every time I read it, rolling their eyes skyward and shaking their heads in disbelief.

The show was going great. My big moment arrived. The tutors were sitting holding their heads, afraid to listen. No sweat. I took my cue and shouted excitedly at Ray Milland, "Er geht in den Keller! Er geht in den Keller!" Perfect, I thought. I glanced at the professors. They were just shaking their heads.

With the show over, one of them came over and said, "Do you have any idea what that line meant, young man?"

"Certainly, I was pointing at Ray Milland and shouting, "There's your killer! There's your killer!"

"I know that's how you read it. And your German was passable."

"Then what's the problem, Professor?" I asked smugly.

"The problem is that your mother had asked you where you had lost your ball and you answered her, pointing at the hero, shrieking at the top of your lungs, 'It's in the cellar. It's in the cellar.' " And he turned on his heel and left. My only thought was, at least the director didn't know the difference.

THINK BIG has always been more than my philosophy of life. It is my *way* of life. I never did see me as small. God gave me a perfectly shaped, well-coordinated body. My approach has been to be as big as I had to be to achieve the goals I set for myself. That's one reason I decided early on in Hollywood to stick to the voice-over profession. I was glad I did.

In the Hollywood TV and film business, they kept viewing me as small, like belonging in a circus. For instance, a top rated comedy show wanted me to walk into a scene smoking a huge cigar with a 6' blonde on my arm. I accommodated my new agent and agreed to meet with the producer because I had worked with him on a few radio shows. I started reading the part and he said right away, "Oh, that's great. You're it."

"Thank you for thinking of me but I just can't do it," I said as respectfully as I could.

"Why not . . . you're perfect for it," he ranted. Then turning to my agent, he ranted some more. "What is it . . . are you holding me up for more money?"

Before my agent could respond I jumped in. "Money has

nothing to do with it. First, I don't smoke and will not do anything that will even hint that smoking is OK."

"OK, forget the cigar. Carry a blankety-blank cane if you want to," he countered loudly.

"Second, I think it is ludicrous to intimate that someone my size would be hauling a six-foot-tall blonde around." And with that I headed for the door. Turning for one last salvo, I said, "If you ever get a part that requires serious acting and isn't a travesty, call me." I turned to my agent and said, "I'll wait for you in the lobby." As I walked through the outer office and down the hall I could hear my agent saying, "Forget the money. Fortunately he's doing quite well, thank you. And he's a pro. He doesn't have to do crap like this. It insults his intelligence."

The louder voice was arguing, "Who the hell does he think he is? Little guys like him are lucky to get work . . . ." By that time I was out of earshot.

I hadn't worked my way through Michigan State for four years and gambled everything I had to make it in Hollywood just to do that kind of work for a living. It was go first-class or nothing. Hollywood was going to see me as a serious, professional actor or I wouldn't play. Many years later Carol Burnett put it a slightly different way. Paraphrasing her words . . . don't let money change your long-range goals. Stay on track. If you are offered something that is not really what you want to be doing long-term, turn down the money and devote full time to the proper direction. My term for that same philosophy is THINK BIG.

A strange series of events occurred that first year in Hollywood. Once in a while I would go to a movie. I went to see Jimmy Stewart and June Allyson in "The Glenn Miller Story." After I got back to my hotel, there were calls for two shows—Six Shooter and Hollywood Star Theater. The star on the first was Jimmy Stewart, and the star on the second was June Allyson. Just a coincidence I figured, at first. But it kept happening. Later the same thing happened with Dewey Martin, Jeff Chandler, Kirk Douglas, Tyrone Power, Joseph Cotten and Frank Sinatra. Talk about a thrill a minute.

Another first took place just about that time. Audiotape came to radio. Until then an E.T. had been used. E.T. stood for Electrical Transcription. It was a 16-inch record. Wire was used briefly, but very little. The first radio show to be taped was a big one and goes down on my list as my favorite to work. It was Gunsmoke, directed by Norman McDonnel and starring Bill Conrad as Matt Dillon, Parley Baer as Chester, Howard McNear as Doc and Georgia Ellis as Kitty.

The first show was taped in March of 1952. It was about a few unsolved murders in Dodge City while a runaway kid, my part, was being cared for by Matt and Chester until his mother arrived. In the end they figured out it was the kid who was murdering all these people—but now he had run away again. His mother, Ginny Gregg, has the final scene with Dillon:

Dillon: How old is he, ma'am?
Mom: About 10 (sniff, sniff).
Dillon: You say his name is William, Mrs. Bonney?
Mom: Yes, Marshall.
Dillon: Does he have a nickname?
Mom: A what?
Dillon: A nickname. What do the other youngsters call him?
Mom: Oh . . . Billy, the Kid.
Theme up and out. End of show.

Gunsmoke was extremely well done. And when the show went to TV, it was highly rated for years.

I thought if I frequented the Curt Massey-Martha Tilton show it would hurry up the Alka-Seltzer session. But no such luck. On the other hand the show was entertaining, and it was a great way to break up a long day. To make it even better, there was another show across the hall called Club 15, starring Bob Crosby and the Modernaires. I was in hog heaven.

Finally, one day in late August, Mr. Owen, during a break in the rehearsal and seeing me in the back of the control room, said the magic words: "Did you get your call for the Speedy session?"

"No, sir. Do you want to give it to me or should I call your secretary?" I asked, trying to sound calm.

"Best you call Dolores. She has all the details and is trying to coordinate everything with Charlie Chaplin, our director [no relation to the Little Tramp]. Why not use this phone to call her, then we'll both know," his humor causing him to snicker loudly.

Dolores gave me the call. Hearing a studio I had never heard of, I wrote it down carefully. She gave me directions, where to park, studio number, time, date and number of spots. I then compared notes with Mr. Owen. "That's a new studio to me but she gave me good directions. I'll see you tomorrow morning at 11."

And I did. I wasn't the least bit anxious. I always get to a session a half-hour early. Also getting there early was the director Charles Chaplin. He was a little ruffled-looking, his sports coat needed pressing, his tie was mostly untied, his hair was a little mussed up, but what a personality! He was always laughing or smiling. And enthusiastic . . . oh my, yes. I was going to like Mr. Chaplin.

Mr. Owen got there with the scripts and the storyboards, also quite early, and the two of them told me what they wanted. The storyboards are like the cartoon strips in the funny paper. They describe pictorially what you will see on the TV screen, with the dialogue printed underneath each picture. They showed Speedy jumping down a staircase of Alka-Seltzer boxes, describing the symptoms of a headache and upset tummy and how Alka-Seltzer would make you feel better.

"Do the voice you did last February, Dick," said Mr. Owen. "Can you remember what you did?"

"Barely, but I think I can come close."

"I've got it in the booth somewhere," said Chaplin. "But let's hear Dick first and go from there."

"Miles liked your enthusiasm, your smile, clarity and articulation, Dick, so keep it clean," said Owen. With that they both went back into the control room.

Chaplin hit the talk-back and slated it and gave me a cue. Off I went.

Charles Chaplin was in full charge in the control room. It was his session. He was the dictator. I knew from my early training I was only as good as my director. I also knew that Chaplin was my kind of director.

"OK, before we listen to the playback, you are three seconds long. You started off OK but then slowed down in the middle." Turning to the engineer he said to both of us, "OK, roll the playback."

He was dead right. What an ear he has, I thought. I nodded that I heard what he had heard. "Give me a second to mark this, please."

"Take your time," came back over the talk-back. I made a few notes, put down my pencil and nodded that I was ready.

Slate, cue, go! Better, I thought, but I can do one better.

"OK, playback," Chaplin says over the speakers.

We all listen. He and Owen confer. "OK, one more. The time is about on but it sounds rushed in some places. Smooth it out, a little less strident, make him likeable. No—make that lovable."

At this point the concentration required is unbelievable. But I know that only perfection will be accepted by this director and that suited me fine.

Slowly it got better and better and then about "take 10" they bought it. Speedy Alka-Seltzer was slowly getting there, and I was loving every minute of it.

On we went to the next spot and the next. The problem for the voice actor is fatigue, voice fatigue. But I was so charged up my voice was getting better, not fatigued. Ninety minutes later we wrapped it up. It had been tough, concentrated, exacting work for two people who knew what they had to have and were going to get it. And they got it. The three of us chatted about the next steps, but I knew now it was just a matter of waiting. Not for the Chaplin team. Now began hours of editing, designing and building sets, stop-motion animation and photography. The work had just begun for them.

The big moment had finally arrived and now, just like that, it was over. I got down to my car, got in, put my key in the ignition, went to start the car, and I was suddenly overcome by fatigue. I literally couldn't turn the key. All I could do was just sit there. Ten minutes passed and feeling halfway decent, I headed back to the hotel, smiling every foot of the way. Talk about lunch tasting good. In fact, I decided I deserved an afternoon off . . . my first since January 7. If that's what giving 110% means, then I'm all for it.

In January of 1953 television was growing rapidly. Those of us in radio could see the demise of our beloved industry slowly taking place, and it was breaking our hearts. Sponsors were taking their money over to the new kid on the block—television.

Speaking of television, you can't believe the shock of turning on a television set and hearing your voice coming back at you. But this told me that the new Alka-Seltzer spots were entering their test market phase and a decision would be forthcoming. And none too soon. With radio shows declining and my decision not to go the film route, my income was also slowly fading. As concerned as I was, I reflected on two things. One was the saying I took with me from Detroit to Hollywood: "When a smaller door closes, a bigger door has already opened." The second thought always turned to THINK BIG. It had never failed me, and I just knew that I was moving in the right direction now. I also believed that the Speedy project was a winner. What I didn't realize then was just how enormous the new television commercial industry was going to be. I was about to find out. It was late January, 1953.

"Dick, this is Dolores Chadwick, Mr. Owen's secretary. Could you be in his office at nine tomorrow morning?"

"Can you tell me what this is about?" I was hoping against hope it was the big news I was waiting for.

"Well, I'm not sure." I detected a slight evasiveness in her voice. "I'm sure it's about Alka-Seltzer, though."

She wasn't going to go any further with the information so I ended with, "Yes, I'll be there at 9 a.m., and thank you."

Actually I was there at 8:45 a.m., just slightly excited. Dolores Chadwick ushered me into Mr. Owen's office. Despite his usual all-business demeanor, he seemed a bit upbeat, too. I scanned his desk looking for a clue—like a contract or something. Nothing. As usual he got right to the point.

"The spots you did tested satisfactorily, Dick. The client has decided to proceed with the project."

"Gosh, that's good news," I said with a big sigh of relief. "That is good news."

"Some new spots are in the mill and should be ready in a few weeks. They will be in color, which will be a first for the industry. Charles Chaplin has left Four Star, and his new company Swift-Chaplin is gearing up for the new series. So it looks as if we're about ready. We will be doing four new spots. If the client is happy with the results, then we'll offer you a new contract at a stipulated annual guarantee paid twice monthly. If the residuals exceed the guarantee, then you will be paid the difference. We'll compute that every three months. How does that sound?"

"Fine," I said, squirming a bit. A poker player I was not. "What's the schedule for doing the spots?"

"Right now we're shooting for the middle of the month. We might have to do it on the weekend because of Country Washburn's schedule. (He was the orchestra leader on the Massey-Tilton show.) We'll also be using the Mellow Men, Bill Lee's group. But we'll keep you posted and give you plenty of notice."

Then he opened a drawer and pulled out a contract. "Here is your new contract that will supersede the old one. Read it over, and if you have any questions, call me and we'll talk about them."

With that, we shook hands and I left. I wanted to pinch myself to make sure what was really happening was true. The Speedy Alka-Seltzer commercials proved to be effective. The prospects were mind-boggling. In a way, though, I was a bit edgy because this contract in my hand was still maybe months from taking effect, and my income was dwindling. A sizable check coming in every two weeks was very important to the free-lance actor who had never known what a regular salary was like. I was fighting the mental battle of insecurity vs. THINK BIG or small door and big door.

Then I remembered a meditation I had seen earlier that month. It said that if I get into the right thought I will demonstrate prosperity. My right thought from that point on was that God was in charge and God was taking care of it.

The subsequent change in my attitude from impatient to relaxed moved everything along smoothly. Two weeks later, on Sunday, March 16, 1953, my 26th birthday, we worked most of the day taping the first Speedy Alka-Seltzer spots.

It was the best birthday present anyone could have given me.

It marked the beginning of a new era in my life. Suddenly I was a pioneer in a new industry that was blossoming right in front of me. I was in demand not only to do radio shows but now TV commercials, especially the latter. The demand meant more income. A lot more income. It also meant I was not to be alone to enjoy it. My parents started looking westward, as did my young brother, who was graduating soon from college. It was about to be a different ball game.

15

Gain Meets Pain

It's amazing how a silly little thing like a contract and a check coming in every two weeks can change the attitude of a freelance actor. Once the commercials began their nationwide run, the dollars suddenly had more zeros tacked on to them. My newfound relaxed attitude toward work suddenly brought many and varied opportunities. One was my first film opportunity, and it was a dilly. First, I was stupid to take it at the daily rate they offered. My reasoning stemmed from the competitiveness of the business and a desire to work and be busy. And to work and be busy in a free-lance environment meant you took anything you could get. In 1953 I was not in a position to turn down anything. Radio shows didn't always include kid parts. Neither did commercials. So when my agent called about this TV film audition I was there. He warned me he wasn't sure how much money he could get me but it was there if I was interested. It was a kid's part, and directors liked hiring me because they didn't have to hire a teacher and a social worker and put up with a stage mother. At that point I could pass as a 10-year-old.

When I got there the not-so-fancy lobby was filled with kids and their mothers, so of course the competitive juices started flowing. When my turn came I was shocked at the shabby office and shabbier furniture. The director had me read several scenes. It was simple stuff, no complicated scenes, all rather straightforward.

"We'll shoot two days," he began, snuffing out one cigarette and reaching for another. "You'd have to go to Western Costume for wardrobe. Nothing fancy—what a kid would wear to school these days. Ever fired a gun?"

"BB gun, 22 rifle, .38 police special."

"OK, you have to shoot a revolver in this thing. Blanks, of course, but you have to look like you don't know much about it. For a pro like you that shouldn't be any problem." That remark, today, would tip me off, along with his phony grin. But not at only 26 years old. I ate it up. Dumb!! All I could think of was beating all those kids and their stage mothers out there in that lobby.

And I did. The money this low-budget operator saved by hiring me was what he was looking for. The best my agent could get was scale, which I think was $55 a day. Of course I could have turned it down, you say. And I say, yeah, and let one of

94

those kids get that part? Are you crazy?

I spent a few hours in wardrobe, more time at his office so he could check wardrobe and I could get a script. It was then that a secretary or assistant asked me to call Screen Actors Guild, Station 16.

"What's that?" I asked.

"Well, hon, you have to be a member of SAG to work film and they want to talk to you."

I called and got Station 16, which was a bossy woman, bored with me and her job. She talked to me as if I were a machine.

"You new in town?"

"No. I've been here a year."

"First film work?"

"Here, yes. But many years in Detroit."

"Belong to SAG back there?"

"Certainly. I had to."

"Doesn't cut it out here. You have to pay another $150 to work out here."

"What do you mean? That's silly."

"$150 or you can't work. Pay it by this afternoon. You got an hour."

"But I belong to . . . ." Click. Station 16 didn't like me much.

I called my agent. He wasn't much help. "Hey son, they got rules. I forgot you didn't belong out here yet. I could've told you. They figure with all the work that's here you gotta pay more than Detroit. That's show biz, kid."

I wouldn't have hated him if he hadn't laughed. "But it's silly to have to run up there in 45 minutes to give them a check."

"Let me call the head man over there. I'm sure he'll let his people bill you. Just stay put a minute."

Two minutes later the phone jingled. It was my agent. "OK, I took care of it. But I'm on the hook for it so don't leave town. Station 16 will call the folks over there. Talk to you later."

One reason I'm even mentioning this job, as insignificant as it was, is to describe how stupid the free-lance actor can be, or has to be, to survive in the business. Another reason is to point up again why I don't like on-camera work and did very little of it after that. In fact, I think only twice more until just a few years ago, which was a special situation. But never again for scale.

My call was for 7 a.m. in makeup in a very cold, dirty studio. Ice-cold smelly makeup in an ice-cold, dirty studio is awful. My dressing room was even dirtier. We started shooting at eight. I don't think they got to my first scene until 11 a.m. But it was a gasser. It was where I had to shoot the gun.

The other actor and I walked through the scene. It called for me to eventually sit on the edge of a desk and threaten him with the gun unless he let me see my big brother or something like that. He asked me during rehearsals if I had ever fired a gun on camera like this, and I made the mistake of saying no. Now this suave, cool-as-a-cucumber actor got a bit frightened and rather nervous. He was fine, almost, until we tried a take and he KNEW I was not going to miss him with that wad in the blank. He KNEW, and he played the whole scene looking straight into the barrel of that revolver, instead of me. The director wanted me to wave it around and gesture with it. You should have seen this poor guy bobbing and weaving with every gesture. It was all I could do not to break up.

So I fired it. I missed him by a cool two inches. Right by his little pink left ear. He was so relieved he almost keeled over. But of course, even with a low budget picture, the director wanted another take. It took the poor makeup man two minutes to soak up his perspiration. This time I figured I would teach him not to sway too far to the right so I missed his little pink right ear by two inches.

"OK, that was very good, people," shouted the director. The damp, pale victim was making his quick exit. "But, I want one more, and this time, Dick, see if you can shoot his hat off. We'll put a wire on it."

I thought he was going to faint. Poor man, now he'd run out of ways to sway. And he couldn't duck or we'd be there all night. After they had installed a wire to the back of his hat, to be yanked at just the right moment, he perched his hat high on his head. That is until just before the call . . . "Action" . . . when the director jumped up and adjusted it, downward.

"Hold real still now," I whispered. "I'll get it."

He wasn't convinced. Neither was I, really. But we had a go at it. And, by golly, the wad hit it dead center. I got only a dab of the wad between his eyes. Hardly enough to fuss about. Needless to say, when we did the close-ups of me, he read his lines from well behind the camera. And for his close-ups . . . the gun was fired straight up.

To this day I can still see his eyes as the moment of the gunshot approached. For the hat trick, they actually crossed! As was typical of the Hollywood scene, I never saw him again.

We worked until 6 p.m. They brought in sandwiches and coffee and then we worked until nine. The next day it was almost the same. I got back to the hotel at seven, had dinner and then decided to take a shower and go to bed. Was I tired, exhausted, or as an experienced professional did I take the whole thing in stride? Believe it or not I fell asleep in the shower. Why I didn't fall I'll never know. I don't remember getting into bed.

I slept for 14 hours. I netted, less my agent's 10%, maybe $70. Put another $80 with it and I was paid up at Station 16, SAG. Neat, huh? That's show biz.

The 8-to-5 knocking on doors, scratching and selling did have its brighter sides. Once in a while a fellow performer would recommend you and it meant work. The Mellow Men performed on our first Alka-Seltzer session. Bill Lee and Thurl Ravenscroft were two of the voices in the group. Thurl is now your friendly and lovable voice of Kellogg's Tony the Tiger and has done tons of Disney voices. But at that time, the Mellow Men were four of the best and busiest voices in Hollywood and sang in all the vocal groups, Norman Luboff Choir, Johnny Mann Singers and many others.

Hearing me sing on the Alka-Seltzer spots, Bill and Thurl recommended me to Gordon Jenkins for his new album called Seven Dreams. Bill Lee was the lead on that famous, best seller.

I had a small part. I was an impatient little kid who was singing, "Are we there yet Mommy, are we there yet Mommy..." and so on. My tag line is kind of whispering in her ear,"Mommy, I have to go to the . . . ." And she says, "All right, let's go," and she and I fade out.

I wanted to impress Mr. Jenkins with my acting ability but I forgot only one thing. We had rehearsed the music while the chorus was on a break so they hadn't heard the scene. I was the only one in the building who couldn't sight-read music and didn't have perfect pitch. These people were pros. I was the amateur. Gordon was satisfied with my rendition after the 10th run-through so he called back the group and we had at it. They were so good he didn't have to rehearse them. They rolled tape. When I got to my part I guess I overdid it a bit. The whole chorus roared with laughter.

"Cut! Cut!" He was fuming. He looked at the chorus, looked at me, then shouted at the top of his lungs, "Damn it, kid, you don't have to go that bad!!"

It took those pros, the best voices in town, six takes— that's SIX—to finally stop laughing. It got to giggle time and some dropped out before I got to the line. I worked with them for years afterward, and it was a standing joke. Thank you, Bill Lee, wherever you are.

Another film opportunity came up, actually a TV film, but this time, with a new agent and attitude, I got some decent money. I was ready to turn it down. If an actor is not prepared to do that the agent has no bargaining point whatsoever. This agent had a great line, "Beals wouldn't get out of bed for that kind of money. And he doesn't have to, thank you."

The show was the Bob Cummings Show, and in addition to

the stars of this show, the great actor named John Litel was also cast for this episode. He and I had a scene that will go down in history as his most painful. I was a little brat he had to baby-sit. We got in an argument and I was supposed to kick him in the shins. Prior to the scene, the assistant director came up and gave him a protective pad to wear under his pants leg. Litel was nervous about my remembering to kick the shin with the pad on it, and rightly so, because the director had directed me to really let him have it full blast. "Give it all you got, Dick," were his exact words.

We rehearsed it a couple of times, just faking the kick. The practiced actor was doing a magnificent job of reacting to the "pain" of the kick. The director made some changes in movements for better camera angles, a funnier payoff to the scene, and Litel got a little confused, I guess. I noticed off the set he was adjusting the shin pad—I figured to get wider coverage or something. Anyway we were all set to shoot the scene and the director called for ACTION.

We made our entrance, went through our argument and I let go the hardest kick possible for a 76-pound spoiled brat. I really caught him flush. His reaction was again magnificent. He writhed in pain, screamed and yelled. I made my exit. The director yelled "CUT," and Litel continued to scream and yell and dance around on one leg. The folks on the set thought he was just being funny, good sports that they were, so they laughed with him. Until someone realized he was in real pain. Then he was surrounded by a whole studio full of people. The nurse pulled up the pants leg, and suddenly a whole studio full of people were running for cover. You should have seen that shin bone. It was puffed up, bleeding and split open something awful. Needless to say, production was halted for a bit. Guess who was in the doghouse for kicking the wrong leg? I knew I hadn't, but nobody was convinced except the director, who defended me to the hilt.

Thirty minutes later the great one came back with a thick bandage under his pants leg and an obvious limp. With a goodly-sized crowd around him the story finally came out. It seems the old pro had taken off the pad to pull up his sagging socks and then carefully put it back, on the wrong leg.

It wasn't often that I watched a show I'd done, but this one I watched. The scene should have won an award.

The public didn't know who was doing Speedy but the industry did. And I was in demand. Maverick, sponsored by Kaiser Foil, was a big hit. Kaiser Foil had developed a little character called the Kaiser Kid. Oscar Mayer put a voice to Little Oscar. The Campbell's Soup Kids had voices. I did all of them.

About that time another important event took place that was to have a long-lasting effect on my life. Forrest Owen invited me to a Big Ten Club luncheon at the Biltmore Hotel in downtown Los Angeles. The Big Ten Club was made up of graduates from the Big Ten schools. The morning of the event he called and had to cancel but had arranged for me to be hosted by a Hugh Tolford, also Michigan State, and treasurer of the Club. The guests of honor were the University of Michigan track team and their coaches. They were competing in a meet with USC and UCLA. Of course, the local coaches and athletic directors were there also.

I was impressed. I was hooked. I was asked to join. I did. For the first time since being in California I felt comfortable with people. Actors were nice to me but we weren't cut from the same cloth. They didn't know a Rose Bowl from an Army-Navy game from a Chuck Davey. These Big Tenners were my kind of people.

From that first meeting, my involvement grew rapidly. The Michigan State Alumni Club put me on the board of directors. The Big Ten Club got me involved on the program committee, which meant that I was the emcee at some of the meetings. I was soon asked to serve on the board of directors, representing Michigan State. Being active in these two organizations put me in constant contact with the businessmen in Los Angeles.

This was the beginning of something that was to give me a new outlook on life and expand my thinking from just acting. The Angels were at it again.

Posing with acting great John Litel, on the Bob Cummings TV show. Later in this scene, Dick kicks Litel, but Litel had the protective pad on the wrong shin. The scene turned out to be more realistic than the director had ever imagined.

At CBS, Hollywood, 1956, with famed author Ray Bradbury and Dick's hero, Ginny Gregg, Hollywood's number one radio actress. The show was the thriller, Suspense.

1953 - Dick visits the set at Swift-Chaplin Studios, where the first "stop-motion" Speedy Alka-Seltzer commercials are being filmed.

16

New Goals - - New Angels

Setting new goals was the tough part. Again, as a free-lance actor, you don't control your working life. But my approach was that with the Alka-Seltzer contract, the new diversified work coming in, and the reputation I had in the industry, I could at least set reasonable goals. Better yet I could control the pressures that were causing my health problems. But how do you set goals? What is reasonable? Where do I start?

This was in the back of my mind, I guess, as I was at CBS one day for a Gunsmoke radio show. A well-known actress was in the cast that day and related what a minister had said in church Sunday. It was as if he was talking to me. He said, "You don't have a health problem. You are taking on mental burdens that are weighing you down. You are trying to solve them instead of turning them over to a higher power who has more answers than you'll ever have." He then went on to give a step-by-step account of how to set positive goals.

Seek and ye shall find. Ask and ye shall receive. As ye sow, so shall ye reap. And so on . . . .

I went to hear him and he started me in the right direction. A few of the things he said really hit home. Such as, "Never say anything about yourself that you don't want manifested in your life." And, "When we love something we give it life and energy." Also, "We attract to us what we fear and we attract to us what we love. Identify to ourselves only that which we want to experience." And then he spoke directly to me when he added, "If you want headaches, then talk all day long to yourself and to others about *your* heartaches and *your* pain and *your* suffering. And that's what you'll attract to yourself." I was suddenly reminded of that early Sunday School phrase that I didn't understand at the time, "Stand guard at the portal of your thoughts."

He closed with a thought that I wrote down as soon as I got home. "Desire Is the Force Behind All Things." And, "By Desire We Grow." So, quietly and privately, I made out my list of "Desires."

1. A new home
2. A poodle
3. Good health
4. Increased business activity
5. Involvement with the business community

These were the first things that crossed my mind, not

necessarily in that order. OK, so it was a start. Another time he spoke on setting goals and explained the Golden Key process. Briefly, the Golden Key says you must be grateful for what you have before you can get new desires. So he suggested that we make out a list of what we have to be grateful for and why. Then we add three things to that list as if we have already received them and why we are grateful for them also. Review that list at least twice daily. So I did.

Being bombarded with this sudden onslaught of positive thinking gave me a new lease on life. The effect on my outlook on life was amazing. Things began to happen.

Forrest Owen called me in for a meeting. As I entered his office I noticed he had my contract on his desk. The first two-year deal was about to run out, but I was pretty sure they would renew.

After some small talk, he told me he was going to be transferred to New York to head up the new Wade office there but wanted to talk to me about the new contract before he left.

"Naturally, Miles is pleased. They've authorized us to offer you a new contract. It's for three years, with the same options but at a slightly higher figure." He handed me the new contract.

I glanced at it, saw the new figure, which seemed fair to me, basically because the usage always exceeded the annual guarantee, so what difference did it make. "Seems fair to me, but I want to take it home and read it."

"Is the money OK?"

"Sure."

"Are you sure? Wouldn't you rather have an escalation clause each year?"

"Yes, I guess I would." A tough negotiator I wasn't.

"Well, how about . . . ," and he named three figures, starting with one higher than the one in the contract, going higher each year.

"OK with me. That would be great."

"All right . . . let me rewrite this to reflect these new numbers. You take that one, pencil in the new numbers, and read it over, and when I have it ready and when Miles approves it I'll call you." Then in mock anger he thumped his desk and said, "You sure drive a hard bargain, Beals."

Two days later I signed a new three-year deal. We shook hands on it, which for me meant more than what was written on that paper. He told me about his new job.

"We've bought some shows that are produced back in New York so I'm heading back to supervise them."

"Which are they?"

"ABC News with John Daly, The Garry Moore Show with a

101

new gal named Carol Burnett and a new show with Robert Q. Lewis."

"And our new Speedy spots will be on them?"

"Yes, sir. Miles is sponsoring the shows. So if you're ever back that way stop by and visit. They'd all like to meet you, I'm sure."

Soon thereafter my agent called me about a shot at a new children's TV series, to be produced by a major book publishing company. The president was in town and wanted to talk to me about it. My agent added, "Money is no object." We met the man at the Beverly Hills Hotel for lunch. I guess he was impressed. He ordered some stills of me in a white tux, which he took back to show his board. My agent worked out a huge deal.

The board must have liked what they saw, for they gave the project the go-ahead and it was to be filmed in New York City.

The highlight of the trip was not the TV pilot. It was ill conceived and poorly planned. But Forrest Owen had visits lined up at the aforementioned shows and I met all the stars and watched then rehearse and do the shows. That was a strange feeling; it put my role in its proper perspective. I knew these people were big stars. Big name stars. Household names. They treated me as if *I* were a star. And I wasn't. My character, Speedy, was a household name, but thank goodness *I* wasn't. I could see what an advantage I had. The voice of Speedy was anonymous and Miles and Wade intended to keep it that way. I was all for it. A private life was just what the doctor ordered, as far as I was concerned.

The trip home took me through Ft. Worth for a few days. What I heard there brought the prospects for that new home closer than my present thinking called for. Dad's business was failing. I was about to have the whole family living with me. I had the added pressure of finding my dad a job in California. All I could think of was two things. That nice, roomy, two-bedroom apartment was going to be overcrowded soon; where was I going to build that house?

Something I read before I left for New York flashed into my mind at that moment. "State specifically what you want and bring all wisdom to this request. Every man receives guidance on what he thinks upon." So I kept my positive thoughts on the solution . . . not the problem. I tried to visualize a pleasant and rewarding job for dad and a dream house that would suit all my needs, whatever they were going to be. And so it was.

I did enjoy life a great deal more. I was busy with my work, active inthe Big Ten Club, and asked to serve as president again in the MSU alumni club. By the time my parents arrived I had three jobs in the automotive business lined up for my dad thanks to friends in the Big Ten Club. He was gainfully employed two days after arriving.

Thanks to the Golden Key, 1956 turned out to be some year. First, the new home. The view was really a view. To the north you could see the Hollywood Hills sign. All of the L.A. Basin was spread out before you. At night it was all lights. On a clear day you could see the mountains around Palm Springs. With binoculars to the southeast you could see Disneyland, which had just opened. I bought the lot and interviewed builders. I picked the top contractor in the area after walking through some of their homes. They listened to my needs and designed a home to fit. We broke ground in July.

Alka-Seltzer was going great guns. Speedy was selling product. There weren't many radio shows left but I was still in demand. Disney had me do a few cartoons. One I did for Warner Brothers won an Oscar. TV commercials were going full bore. I was busy and making good money.

Two days before Thanksgiving I had my sixth attack of something like appendicitis. It was always diagnosed as an inflammation of the abdominal wall. For the sixth time, the doctor couldn't find the problem. It didn't hurt where it was supposed to but he thought it was my appendix, so he ordered tests. The barium test said retrosecal appendix, which means twisted upside down and backwards.

The house was two weeks from completion. I was chairman of the Big Ten Club Dinner for Champions on December 29 for the Iowa Rose Bowl team and 1,200 alumni. The next day Wade Advertising called and announced that Miles Laboratories wanted me to make a surprise appearance at their national sales meeting December 17 in Elkhart, Indiana, the company's headquarters. The doctor wanted me in the hospital, NOW! "What you've thought were abdominal infections all these years were six attacks of appendicitis. The next attack could be serious." I told him I would go in January 1 and no sooner. He begrudgingly set the date of January 2, 10:00 a.m.

So I moved into the house on December 7. I immediately bought an eight-week-old black toy poodle, which was promptly named Silhouette.

The Miles trip was exciting and very rewarding. They had to keep me sequestered in the hotel to make it a big surprise. The salesmen really brought down the house. That same night I was back on the train, taken to a hotel and out to an early flight the next day.

The dinner was a howling success. On the 30th I called Forrest Owen, who was back in Hollywood now heading up the Wade office, and told him about the scheduled surgery. He was the only one outside the family to know.

The surgery was a breeze. The only complaint I had was the food. I got cold, dry, tasteless sliced turkey every lunch and every dinner for three days. On the fourth day I complained hesitantly to my doctor.

"Doctor, wasn't the surgery successful?"

"Certainly. You're in great shape. What's the trouble? Are you hurting?"

"Well, no. But why can't I eat normal food? I had to watch what I ate before the surgery, now I can't get anything but cold, dry, tasteless sliced turkey. After Thanksgiving and Christmas I've had it up to here."

"That's silly. You can order anything you want. Steak, shrimp, lobster, anything on the menu. You know that."

"Well, I ordered it but all I get is turkey and . . . ." With that, he bolted for the door saying, "Oh my God, what have they done?"

They had been giving the ulcer patient across the hall anything he wanted and he was getting sicker by the day. By mistake, I was getting what he should have been getting.

The goals I had set for 1956 had been met. I had my beautiful new home, my poodle, my much improved health, new business opportunities and active involvement with top business people. Happy 1957. It was time to set new goals. THINK BIG!

17

New Contract - - New Life

Recuperating from the appendix surgery went quickly, what with a little black poodle to train, a new house to landscape and lost time to make up at the recording studios. The doctor finally released me two weeks after I got home, which was about right for me. It hurt to ride in a car and I tired easily. I couldn't have survived a radio session if I had wanted to.

The nice thing about staying home with nothing to do was that it gave me time to dream a little bit and start setting new goals. The Golden Key philosophy worked for me. There was no doubt about it. I just expanded my list. I included the things I had wanted and had received on my list of things for which I was grateful and why, then added some new ones.

The work category came first but I had to make up my mind which direction I wanted to go. Radio was dying out slowly but surely. Alka-Seltzer sales were climbing and my contract with Wade Advertising had a year to go. You would think something like a contract renewal is automatic if sales are up but such was not the case in this business. I did want a contract renewal and more money, but more importantly, I wanted more business activity from a wider variety of sources. So that was No. 1 on my list.

Two, I wanted more involvement in the business community. I liked these people, such as those I was working with in the Big Ten Club and Michigan State alumni club. I also wanted to be steadily building up a reputation with these people, in case I ever wanted to break away from acting and go into business. Three, sports kept flashing into my mind. So I added, "Involvement with sports and coaching." I really didn't know which way to go with that one so I just put it down and let a higher power work it out. Four was flying. In the back of my mind I had always wanted to fly an airplane, but at only 4'6'' and not being too strong, something told me to forget it. But not now. It went on the list.

The list was reviewed at least once a day. I put reminders where only I would see them just to key my thought to the list. This system worked for me. And taking stock of my surroundings and my work reminded me of that fact too. The system, the thought pattern—it worked if you let it. I believed in it. I knew it would work now and forever. THINK BIG!

It was about this time that I became acquainted with the Hollywood Police Department, or they became acquainted with me. It was after a tough recording session and I was heading home. I was driving my new 1955 Chevrolet and, as in my other cars, I had my cushions in there to prop me up and a special portable device Terry had designed to extend the pedals. Suddenly I noticed in my rear-view mirror that a police car had me in its sights. It was right on my tail.

While one officer was tailing me the other was checking the hot sheet and was on the mike with someone. Heading south on Vine Street, I approached Santa Monica when the light turned amber and then red. I stopped smoothly with the police car tucked in right behind me. They were looking me over real good, certain they had a juvenile out for a joyride in a stolen car. I decided to look busy. My windshield was a bit dirty so I decided to test out my newfangled device called the windshield washer. I turned it on and pushed the "wash" button. To say it was a bit out of adjustment is putting it mildly. The spray missed my windshield completely, missed my car completely, but did a beautiful job of covering the police car's windshield, completely.

Laugh? I thought I'd collapse. The light changed to green but I couldn't stop laughing long enough to drive. I didn't know quite what to do. Then I noticed that the officers were in hysterics. I lifted both of my hands, shrugged my shoulders, all the time looking at them in my rearview mirror. When sanity finally prevailed the driver waved me on, the other officer saluted, I saluted back and headed home.

The key to making the Golden Key work for me is not limiting myself to one source for answers. I imagine myself in the center of a sphere. I am totally surrounded by people, ideas, events, opportunities. Answers therefore could come from anywhere, from people I don't even know, which has usually been, no, has *always* been the case. Such was the case for item No. 1 on my list. When I was ready for action, and not before, career opportunities came at me one after another. Some worked, some didn't, but I pursued each one full out.

A new medium was just beginning to move into the spotlight, the TV cartoon series. The people who were first in line were radio actors. In 1957 only a handful of companies were geared up to produce that kind of volume but work was plentiful. Alka-Seltzer was using Speedy more and more. Radio, although dying slowly, still provided me with plenty of work.

Shortly thereafter Forrest Owen called me and set up a meeting for the next morning. This usually meant contract renewal time. He also told me they were going to take some pictures. For what purpose he didn't say. So with my nice dark brown suit on I showed up. As usual, once I was in his office he got right to the point.

"I have a new contract for you. We think it is fair." With that he handed it to me.

It was for more money, substantially more. It covered more avenues of utilizing Speedy, such as a manikin, sales meetings and others.

"Where this bothers me a little," I began, choosing words carefully, "is that the usage is figured at SAG scale. I want more than scale. Actors all over town are getting over-scale. I deserve the same."

"All right, I can go for over-scale. You are not a scale actor. You work hard and produce results. Anything else?"

"Yes, it's only fair that the salary figure should be higher for each of the next three years of the contract. I've earned it. This is my fifth year as Speedy and I've done my darndest to make the whole thing work. The usage might more than cover it anyway. I appreciate the escalation clause but the base figure should be higher."

"How much higher?"

I popped up with a figure, which he added to his other notes. "Anything else?"

"No."

"I will recommend these changes. I agree with your logic. OK?"

"OK!"

"Now several things to be discussed. First, we will have the photographer here in a few minutes. We want your picture holding a glass of the product. It will be distributed to the Miles salesmen at a regional sales meeting in Las Vegas in September at the new Tropicana Hotel. You are invited."

I guess I was visibly excited.

"Number two, you will probably be traveling more for us. We might be recording you back in Chicago. The writing is being done back there and the TV department is back there, so it's easier to record you back there than to bring the whole crew out here."

We took the pictures and had lunch.

Two events occurred that told me the No. 2 item on my list was working. A few of the Big Ten Club officers invited me to lunch. In short, they told me they wanted me to be very much involved in the Club, be the permanent chairman of the Dinner for Champions and help them with programs. The problem was that they couldn't put me up for election as an officer until 1960. They rotate the presidency among the ten schools and Hugh Tolford was then president and he was from MSU. So if I didn't mind they would put me on ice for a few years.

I didn't mind at all. My contacts with the business community were growing rapidly. Some of the business leaders were calling on me to help them with public relations, they assigned me speaking engagements, I wrote ad copy and edited newsletters, all for a substantial fee. It was working out just right.

An Alka-Seltzer toast to the Speedy manikin, with a taped message from Speedy, about to be placed in supermarkets around the country.

18

Two New Loves

Sports, coaching and flying popped into my life quickly. Again, quite by accident and going along with my sphere theory, it came from a direction I hadn't anticipated. The company that built my home was headed up by Bud Plone. He asked me to compile a list of complaints and when it was sizable call him and he'd come up with some workmen and take care of the problems. I did and he did. He also brought his 10-year-old son, Steve, with him that Saturday. The son was wearing a Little League uniform. His team was the Beavers.

Jokingly Bud said, "I wish you could teach him how to hit. He's having an awful time. He keeps backing away."

Embarrassed, the youngster said, "Well, I'm not the only one, Dad. No one else is hitting either."

"Hitting shouldn't be that tough," I countered. "Let me get a bat and a tennis ball and we'll go to the vacant lot next door."

Bud assigned the jobs to the workmen and he and his son followed me to our new "practice field." I started my seminar on hitting with Steve.

That was the beginning of 17 years of coaching Little League, Pony League, high school and semi-pro baseball teams, and Pop Warner and high school football teams. This initial Little League encounter also introduced me to flying. The sphere concept worked again.

One day at practice with Steve's team and I was suddenly their new assistant coach. Steve's dad, and the manager, Joe Tymczyszyn, were dedicated parents, but they knew nothing about baseball. Soon because of conflicts in their working schedules, I had myself a Little league team. Joe's conflict was a job in Seattle. He had to certify a new airplane, made by Boeing, called a 707. Joe was the FAA's No. 1 chief engineering test pilot. When he finished testing the 707, he called me and took me flying, introducing me to the owner of a flight school. My flying career was under way. All this happened within six months of putting my requests on my new Golden Key list. And the people responsible for this personal growth, and prayers being answered, were unknown to me at the time.

In Little League baseball, sometimes I got a little too excited about winning and losing. But there are the heartwarming stories that live forever, long after the scores and wins and losses are forgotten.

Mike Burke was the smallest youngster on the team. He was

almost nine and had a slight speech impediment. He came up to me after practice one day with his mother.

"Missther Bealsth, I want to be a tetcher."

"A what, Mike?"

"A tetcher."

"Oh I see, you want to be a catcher, huh?"

"Yeah, I mean, yesth thir."

"Do you think you can handle all that equipment? It's pretty heavy. Have you ever worn a mask?"

"Yesth thir. I can wear my frienth's. He's in the majorths."

"It's OK with me, Mike." Then to his mother I said, "He has to wear a protective cup, even at practice, so stop by Sportsville and get him one. Tomorrow we'll give him a try at catching."

"A protective cup?" she asked politely.

"Yes, a protective cup. Phil Bailey at Sportsville will have them. See you tomorrow, Mike." And off he went with his mother.

Next day up drove Mike with his mom. She gave me a big grin and waved as he bounced out of the car with his new protective cup, heavily taped to his *nose.*

A new Alka-Seltzer contract, a membership in the University Club, a leadership role in the Big Ten Club, a free-lance marketing consultant to my friends in the business community, an active role in teaching and coaching sports, a student pilot and many new sources of income . . . the Angel Voices had been active indeed. When I looked back at where I had been in 1951 and where I was in 1958 it was unbelievable. The boost in confidence was certainly gratifying. But it was time to take stock and make a decision. Like what direction was best, acting or business or both? Could I pursue both without hurting my main source of income, acting? Up until now acting had always come first. But business meant daily activity, action, meetings, planning, working with people and competing. I liked that. Sitting around waiting for the phone to ring can be deadly for an actor. But I knew from my work in the Big Ten Club I could compete in this area.

Decision? Listen for the Angel Voices and THINK BIG. In no time at all things began to pop. I had more opportunities from which to pick and choose than I knew existed. I decided to look into anything and everything.

Remember the "sphere" concept I described before? It calls for the thought that you are in the very center of a sphere. Therefore you are surrounded by ideas, people, and things instead of being on just one plane. It enforces the belief that we need not look to only those people we know for answers.

110

Answers have always come to me from people I didn't even know and like a shot out of the blue. We never know and should never question from where answers may come. It's all out there for us if we'd only let it flow. And did things start to flow?

Quite by accident I met a young attorney named Fio Lopardo. He turned out to be, over the years, a major influence in my life. He got me involved with some of his clients who needed public relations, advertising, or whatever. As a new young attorney he got involved with many new fledgling companies and he immediately involved me. In fact he had me appointed to the board of directors of a couple of them.

At the same time, another Big Ten Club friend, Warren Dunnell, came from out of nowhere with a shocker. For years he had made paper toilet seat covers, but now he was embarking on something new. It was a foam plastic cup that keeps hot things hot and cold things cold.

"I'm putting together a new company to handle this. I'm going to need a name for the company, a name for the product, advertising material and sales help just for starters. Can you help me?"

"I'd love to, Warren. Can you tell me what they call this new cup. What's it made of?"

"It's made from polystyrene beads. You just pour these tiny white beads into a mold and cook them. They expand and out pops a cup. It has superefficient insulating properties. It will revolutionize the market."

"Sure. Count me in."

"Oh, I forgot to mention it. You're on my new board of directors. I'm also adding you to my Sani-Gard board. OK?"

Glunk. "Sure," I said.

Another new world started creeping into the entertainment industry. I first heard about it in a strange way. I was coaching the Beavers one night and, as usual, leaning up against the fence next to the dugout. A voice behind me said, "Can you have dinner with me tonight after the game?"

I turned and there was an executive from Wade Advertising in Chicago. He was the last person I expected to see at a Little League ball game. Especially since he was in research and not TV production or the creative department. Nor was he an account executive.

"Gordon, what are you doing here? How did you find me?"

"I called your home and got directions. My plane leaves at 9:30 tonight. A real live red-eye. I thought after the game we could have dinner."

So we did, improperly dressed as I was. It was during dinner that he got serious for a moment. "Dick," he began, then paused to weigh carefully his words, "We made a decision to-day that will either be the worst decision in the history of television or the best."

I said nothing. I was thinking Speedy, of course. But Gordon Maltby wouldn't be here to talk about Speedy. After another bite or two he continued. "We bought a TV show for the fall about cavemen."

"Cavemen?"

"Yes, a comedy show. It's about two couples and their dinosaur or something like that. Two men named Hanna and Barbera sold our people on it. And Miles just bought it today. The whole thing."

"Bill Hanna and Joe Barbera?"

"Yes. That Barbera puts on quite a show."

"I know them both. They did the Tom and Jerry cartoons at MGM. Very creative people."

"I hope you're right. But cavemen? And a comedy show? I just don't know what the public is going to think. I hope it works."

"What's it called?"

"The Flintstones."

The new word in the industry was TV cartoons. Joe and Bill were the pioneers, and Flintstones became the first prime-time adult cartoon show. The trick was to make cartoons for TV at a price the sponsors could afford. And Joe and Bill did it. They were followed by many others and suddenly the voice people who were doing commercials were doing cartoon voices. Here we went again!

For me, this period in my life was like a dream come true. It was just what I had in mind when I added it to my Golden Key list, and here it was, bigger than life. I was busy. Speedy continued to be the No. 1 spokesman on television. Radio shows continued, though a far cry from the earlier days. The advertising business was just enough to keep me occupied, the Big Ten Club was a real joy because of the association with the top business executives, and Little League was about to explode onward and upward.

The Big Ten Club had a few pluses I haven't mentioned yet. First, the Big Ten Club was closely allied with the Tournament of Roses because of the Big Ten's contract for the Rose Bowl game. Getting to know the Tournament folks and being included in many of their functions was a pleasure. They were a class act. Second was getting to know the coaches, athletic directors, faculty reps and executives of all the Big Ten schools. These were my kind of people; I was in seventh heaven. At our annual Dinner for Champions, as chairman, I got to know the players from the various schools, too. One in particular, I got to know quite by accident. Accident . . . as in major collision.

Illinois was in the Rose Bowl and we were honoring them in the Biltmore Bowl. I was running around like crazy trying to find out if Bob Hope was going to make it or not when wham, I collided with a huge rock of granite, maybe 6'3'', 240 pounds. It was obviously a football player and he just stood there and stared at me. I bounced back a few feet and for some silly reason decided to attack.

"Why the heck don't you watch where you're going?" I shouted angrily. This was kind of dumb because he actually had been standing still.

"Uh-h-h, are you OK...sir?"

"Yes, I'm fine. Are you looking for your seat or what?"

"No sir...I was looking for more milk. Could I have some more? Please? Sir?"

"Sure, I'll get you some more. Where are you sitting?"

"Right over there, sir," he said pointing. "Thank you, sir."

Then as my head cleared, I recognized him. It was Dick Butkus.

19

Cartoons Explode

"Dr. Hall will see you now, Mr. Beals," said the blasé nurse. She wasn't about to believe that at 4'6", I expected to get an FAA 3rd class medical certificate.

"You?" she smirked, looking down over her glasses.

I looked around behind me and said, "No, it's for my dog down here," glancing down to a spot I knew she couldn't see without getting up from her desk. Once I got her up I said, "Gosh, he was here a minute ago."

Now she *was* ticked. "You'll have to fill out this form," she said. "Bring it back to me when you're finished."

Next, we went to my favorite test, the eye chart. I know she dimmed the lights on purpose to make it tougher. She kept barking the orders. No sense of humor at all. Read this line, cover up the other eye, read that line, the next, the next, and I just kept going down and down the chart.

She knew—she seemed positive—I had memorized the chart in advance. So she got a pointer and had me read the letters as she tapped the chart. Finally, in desperation and with renewed anger, she gave up. I wanted to get her to say aloud the test indicated 20/15 in a dim light.

Now I followed her down the corridor to see the good Doctor Hall. His name was one of three on a list supplied by Lind Flight Service.

Without a word she opened the door to the doctor's office, let me pass, then closed the door firmly.

Dr. Hall was friendlier. He reached out over his desk to shake hands as he pointed to a chair. "Mr. Beals, nice to meet you. Sit down, please. I hope my nurse didn't annoy you too much. She has her good days and her bad days."

"I lose my patience sometimes, Doctor, when people assume one has to be six feet tall to do anything. I tried to be pleasant and joke about it but I guess it was the wrong approach. Next time, I'll get mad."

"No, please don't. Keep joking about it." He chuckled a bit, then picked up the test results off the clipboard and quickly reviewed them. "Well, you're in good health. Your eyes are the best we've ever seen here. Mrs. Everett couldn't believe *her* eyes, or your eyes, as the case may be. No pun intended. Promise me you'll take care of them."

I nodded. He put down the papers, leaned forward in his chair, clasped his hands on the desk and looked me straight in the eye. It was serious time. "OK, Mr. Beals, stand by for my little speech. Three things will get you killed in an airplane. One, disregard for the weather. Two, lack of thorough preparation for your flight. Three, fatigue. That's why more doctors get killed in airplanes than anyone else. We are autonomous in a hospital, in an operating room, in our offices. We think we can dictate that the weather will not harm us. We think we can figure things out as we go along and solve any problem. So we don't plan properly. And three, we don't recognize fatigue. Through internship we are on our feet sometimes 36 hours at a stretch. We are always tired." Now he pounded his desk with authority. "You CANNOT FLY AN AIRPLANE PROPERLY IF YOU ARE FATIGUED." He leaned back in his chair, gathered his thoughts, then said crisply, "Do you have any questions about any of this?"

"No, I just thank you for saying it. I really appreciate it."

He got up, reached across the desk to shake hands and said warmly, "I admire you for taking up flying. I'm proud of you. Be a good pilot."

I smiled and headed out the door. About three feet down the hall I heard him say, "Don't forget your dog." I liked him.

Airplane instructors are patient people. Dave Varnum was no exception. Fortunately I was in no hurry to solo. I just enjoyed every minute of it and gradually got the hang of it. We had one good laugh though. About my second or third session he told me to handle the mike. The day before, with bad weather at Santa Monica Airport, I spent my required hour in the tower and became familiar with what they were saying and why. Knowing this, David prepared me for my big moment.

"Now don't get nervous. Think of what you're going to say, don't yell, press the mike button and say it." About then he realized how I made my living and he almost fell out of the still-open door.

"Relax, friend," I chuckled. "I promise you I won't get nervous in front of a microphone." Then I gathered my thoughts, took a deep breath and pushed the button. "Santa Monica Ground Control, Cessna 5869 Echo, Lind, taxi for takeoff."

"Good morning, 69 Echo, taxi runway 21, wind calm."

"Sixty-nine Echo."

We were taxiing up the hill when the tower came back quietly with, "Did you enjoy your visit yesterday?"

"Yes, sir. Thank you."

After the run-up Dave told me to stay in the pattern. I switched frequencies and gave them a call. "Santa Monica Tower, Cessna 5869 Echo ready to go, we'd like to stay in the pattern."

"Roger 69 Echo, taxi into position and hold."

Add power in a bit, taxi to the double line, nose wheel on the center line, slide my new shoe extensions up the rudder pedals, and depress the top of the pedal, which applies the brakes. Sit there and wait. Another plane was rolling out at the far end.

"Piper 28 Tango clear when able, contact ground. Sixty-nine Echo cleared for takeoff." Around and around and around. Staying in the pattern is hard work but as coaches will tell you, "Repetition builds confidence."

The third time, as we were going past the gas pumps, the plane slowed for some unknown reason, so I started to add power. Then I noticed Dave's feet were on the brakes and he was fussing with his seat belt. I was wondering what was wrong when he said those now famous words.

"OK, you try a couple by yourself now." He climbed out and then before shutting the door he leaned back in. "Without me in the plane, it's going to climb like mad. Good luck. Have fun."

I had always been apprehensive about soloing, which meant I wasn't ready, but now that the moment had come it didn't faze me except for a few butterflies. The pattern process was well imprinted in my mind so I just had to do it one more time and concentrate on the things Dave had taught me. I taxied back, waited my turn, they instructed me to taxi into position and hold, and then came the magic words, "69 Echo, cleared for takeoff."

I don't remember much except that it did climb faster. I was at 1,000 feet by the time I was usually at 600 feet. Power back to 2,100, carb heat on, look for traffic, contact the tower. They came back with, "Six-niner Echo you are number three to land. Follow the yellow 150 turning base. Extend your downwind one mile past the freeway."

"Six-nine Echo." Great. Now I had something new to do. I tried to measure my mile accurately, but in the excitement I forgot he said freeway. I measured it from the field. I eased back on the power, turned final, pulled on two notches of flaps and headed in for my first landing, alone. I immediately noticed that my miscalculation on the downwind leg had caused a slight calamity. A plane on the runway in a "hold" position was getting off the runway. This meant the tower had expected me to extend longer but knowing that I was soloing they just had the other pilot get out of the way. Nice of them. The landing? So-so, I guess. Nothing to write home about. I taxied back to the gas pumps to a smiling instructor.

He opened the door and shook my hand. "Congratulations, you just did something you can never do again in your life. Solo for the first time. OK, try another one and get that wheel back." Slam went the door, and off I went.

Now that I was a grizzled veteran I spoke with much greater authority on the mike. Back came the tower. "Going to try it again, huh, Speedy?" Now how did they find out about that?

"Yes, sir. Six-nine Echo ready for takeoff."

Off I went, and this time there was even more traffic but this time I extended properly. And this time I decided to get that wheel back, really back. For the first time I heard the stall warning buzzer just before the tires went *tweak, tweak.* I rolled out past the gas pumps and there was David applauding like crazy. I picked him up and we taxied back to our tiedown area. In the office it was all pats on the back, congratulations and handshaking. I felt great.

It would be nice to report that I went on to bigger and better things with my flying, but it was not to be. Over the holidays I gave it considerable thought and decided not to continue. Flying was exciting, it was a challenge, it gave me a sense of accomplishment, especially at 4'6" and 75 pounds, but it all came down to how I was to use flying. It was expensive and really I had no place to go, except a breakfast or luncheon flight somewhere. I couldn't use it in my business so there was no tax advantage. I firmly believed one had to stay current, but I didn't want to fly just to stay current—that was no fun. In fact, it could be a drudgery. The other thing that bothered me was the caliber of planes available to the renter. They were old, with old equipment and the prospect of newer planes was remote. Joe Tymczyszyn agreed. "These people have to scratch for profit. Very few have the funds to buy new airplanes."

Cartoon shows soon dominated my work load. Two series came up; one, especially was truly exciting. The first was Davey and Goliath, which still ran 20 years later. I was Davey and Hal Smith was Goliath, my trusty dog. It was a cute show with a religious theme.

The second show was written and produced by the most creative man I've ever known, Ken Snyder. He was a creative director of note with a big advertising agency and left his post to put his brainchild on TV. It was called The Funny Company and was sponsored by Mattel Toys. I had the lead as Buzzer Bell, a bright, energetic 10-year-old type, and played another role called Shrinking Violet, a shy, demure, five-year-old girl.

Hanna-Barbera was a busy place, too, and like the old expression, I spent half my life there. There were Flintstones, The Jetsons, Frankenstein, Jr., Squiddly Diddly and many others. Joe Barbera used me almost exclusively. In fact, once he almost used me too much.

I got a call for three Flintstones episodes. I was there early, as usual, found the scripts on the conference table in the studio and noticed there were five children's parts, cleverly named Boy Scout #1, Boy Scout #2, Boy Scout #3, Boy Scout #4 and Boy Scout #5. I didn't know which one I was. Finally Alan Reid, Mel Blanc, Jean Vander Pyle and Bea Benadaret wandered in, followed by the ubiquitous Joe Barbera.

"Joe, who am I today?"

"Hi, Dickie." (To this day I'm still Dickie.) "You're the boy scout."

"But which one, Joe?"

"There's only one. You're 'the' Boy Scout."

Alan Reid (Fred Flintstone) pipes up, "Joe, there are five boy scouts in my script."

Joe checks his script. "Hmmmmm. Hey, you're right. Guess you're all five, kid. You're a pro. You can handle it."

Mel Blanc (Barney) chipped in with, "This will be a TV first. I'm glad I'm here to see this." What made his line funny was that he said it in his Bugs Bunny voice, which always cracked me up.

Five voices are possible to do if there are other people in the scene. But in this story the five kids talked to one another for two full pages. And boy scouts are generally the same age. So I had a problem.

What I ended up doing was conjuring up five different Little Leaguers whom I'd coached. On the script, I replaced the numbers with the kid's names, which triggered my memory as to what they looked and sounded like. In some cases I drew tiny sketches of their faces in front of the lines to emphasize thin, fat, tough, weak, happy, etc.

On an HB show, or any cartoon show for that matter, we have one table reading, then it's up to the separate cast mikes for a voice-level check for the engineer. Then they roll tape and we do it. During the table reading I had time to try some things. Then Mel gave me some ideas, and Jean did too. By recording time, I was ready for the history books. Kind of.

Thank goodness for tape and Joe's great ear. We did only a few pickups (lines done over), but when we were finished, Joe was satisfied that there were five different boy scouts in the scene. Afterward I gave Joe my script with all the sketches to give to the animators. I saw the show weeks later and, by golly, they had used them as guides.

To this day when I see Joe, he says, "Hey, there are my favorite Boy Scouts. Hi, Dickie."

An Alka-Seltzer session turned out to be a classic, too. The date of the recording was important. It was October 15, 1962. For a Dodger fan, that was just after they blew the last four games of the season, allowing the Giants to tie and then beat them in the playoff. The Giants were now up against the Yankees in the often-delayed World Series—often been delayed due to inclement weather. That very day, the Giants and Yankees were playing at Candlestick.

Involved in the session were two pros. One, Shep Menkin, who did the Western Airlines Bird, "The only way to fly." Two, Paul Winchell, superb ventriloquist and veteran voice actor. Of course, I'm doing Speedy. We had rehearsed the first spot for a while when Charles Chaplin hit the talk-back and told us to relax for a moment. "We have to check a line in the script with Elkhart." That meant company headquarters.

Because we were all pros, the engineer, Don Thompson, left the mikes open. But Paul Winchell couldn't stand the boredom. With a wink to Shep and me he casually leaned against his music stand. In his best ventriloquist voice, he began the dialing of a telephone and the ringing of a telephone, which was answered by a man's voice. On the other end of the line was a hysterical woman. Paul was doing all these sounds and voices without so much as moving lip one! The woman was talking to her psychiatrist. Her lurid stories were getting worse by the minute.

The nine or 10 people in the booth gradually became aware of the conversation, especially Charlie and Don. They looked at each other, then at us, and Charlie made motions as if to ask us if we could hear it, too. We, of course, shook our heads no.

Don listened for a second. He knew that above the acoustical ceiling panels hanging on T bars were many phone lines and mike cables. Accidents like this *were* possible. We could only read lips, but he indicated to Charlie he'd fix it. He grabbed the two plugs in the patchboard and reversed them.

When Paul saw this, he immediately switched to the play-by-play of the World Series game between the Giants and the Yankees. The game was a barn-burner. But Paul had a problem: he didn't know a thing about baseball. He had Russ Hodges, slightly inebriated, doing the game, Mickey Mantle breaking his leg, Lou Gehrig playing first. Babe Ruth was in there, as was Leo Durocher, at that moment still a coach for the Dodgers. Boy, was it an exciting game!

Every time Don Thompson touched anything in the booth—anything—Paul returned to the psychiatrist-woman conversation or the ball game. Only one man in the booth knew anything at all about baseball. He sat there with a puzzled look on his face that said, "Babe Ruth??? Lou Gehrig??? Leo Durocher???"

Finally it got so exciting that they took a vote in the booth and it was 7-3 for the ball game.

Paul let it go on for at least five agonizing minutes but he was running out of lurid ideas and ball players. Finally a script girl from Charlie's office went over to the patchboard and asked, "What does that knob do?"

"Nothing! NOTHING!" screamed the exasperated Don Thompson.

Undeterred, she made a fist and hit it. Paul stopped cold. Absolute quiet. We never told them until now.

20

Ill Winds Blow

A voice from the past planted a seed that would take a few years to sprout, though germinate it finally did. It was a surprise long-distance phone call from attorney Fio Lopardo.

"You're calling from where?"

"Escondido."

"I've heard of it but where is it exactly?"

"San Diego County, 15 miles east of Oceanside, 30 miles north of San Diego. In God's country."

"Big law office, huh?"

"Small law office. When are you coming to see me?"

"When can we have a golf game? Any good courses down there?"

"How nice of you to ask. I just won my first big case. Bunch of partners suing for ownership of a country club and my client won. It's private, but we can play it anytime."

"What's it called?"

"Pauma Valley Country Club. It's about 30 minutes from here."

On a 94-degree August day, we played the manicured layout. Of more importance, though, I immediately became lovingly attached to Escondido. It reminded me somewhat of Birmingham. It was the small town I had been looking for since leaving my old hometown. My work was in Hollywood, granted. But there was something there in that small town that I liked. Since leaving Birmingham I had never been able to live in a community. L.A. is not a community. It is a series of shopping centers. Escondido was a community. Yes, a seed was planted.

My acting career was going smoothly and work was plentiful. The Funny Company was in its final stages and here came another Ken Snyder series called Roger Ramjet, in which I played three kids, Yank, Doodle and Dan. Someone else played Dee.

Add to that my relationship with Wade Advertising and Miles Laboratories. In '61 they wrote me a five-year deal with a lot more money. I was sailing, literally.

In 1964, however, storm clouds appeared. Wade was about to lose the Alka-Seltzer account—worth about $12 million a year in billings—to Jack Tinker and Partners. Tinker was telling the world that Speedy Alka-Seltzer would be dropped. I didn't want to believe it but everything I heard from Wade confirmed my worst fears. On September 1, Miles officially appointed Tinker and on September 2, I received the following letter from Forrest Owen:

Dear Dick:

I'm taking over the duties of the treasurer, Laddie Francl, today because I wanted to write you a personal note as our stewardship of the Alka-Seltzer business comes to a close. Hereafter, your contacts will be with Jack Tinker and group or with Miles direct.

Obviously I have no knowledge of their plans for Alka-Seltzer except that they did make a major presentation to Miles yesterday, which I presume included their first creative efforts.

You know how I feel about Speedy and how I feel about you personally. We're all hoping the past success of Speedy will cause everyone concerned to continue in some form or other. In any case, we have been damn proud of the character and your contributions toward his success.

I'm not going to say good-bye because I'll see you from time to time, obviously in Pasadena on New Year's Day, but if not there, in one of the many saloons you frequent.

And, the very best of good luck to you always.

Sincerely,
Forrest Owen

I'll quote only a small portion of my response:

A successful project is always a team effort. However, I have always maintained that your initial direction and guidance was the most vital to the project and most valuable to me personally. Without it, Speedy would have faltered.

It was a sad time. Twelve exciting years as a top corporate spokesman. Twelve years from being frightened and lost in a scary new town with nothing to do but knock on unfriendly doors. Oh yes, my contract would go on through most of 1965 with weekly checks coming in, but Speedy was a has-been and it hurt. I loved doing it. It was time to set new goals.

Escondido continued to be a thought for the future. I bought a 16-acre site in nearby Valley Center suitable for a grove. I decided to syndicate it with four of my friends in the Big Ten Club, keep 20% for myself and manage it. My friends liked it so much that all five shares were gone instantly. I planted orange trees on the acreage, named it PIMMS WEST, an acronym for Purdue, Iowa, Michigan, Michigan State and Northwestern, and we were in business.

It was at this time that another valuable real estate lesson was brought home loud and clear. Again it was something I read, brought home by another Angel Voice, Charles Escallier, one of my Little League coaches and a successful real estate salesman. My beautiful Baldwin Hills home was slowly losing its appeal. I had endured the cold ocean breezes long enough; I wanted to live in a community instead of a shopping area, and I wanted warmer climes. I researched the situation and discovered a lovely residential area in Downey. I found a nice house, bought it, then set about to selling my first one.

I tried to keep in mind that in the perfect plan unfolding for me, a buyer was as much in need of my perfect home as I was in need of selling it. It would happen when I could mentally release it and turn it over to God.

I defined this point as when I stopped saying "my house." Let it go. Think of it as belonging to the next owner.

It made sense, so I did just that. Then Charles Escallier came up with great counsel as far as pricing was concerned. "Pretend you are walking down the street and you see this house. You go in and you like it. You compare prices with other homes in the neighborhood and then decide what you would like to pay for it. That's your price. Stick with it. Firm."

The toughest part of this whole thing was getting egos out of the way. I found that there are people who want to get more for their house than their neighbors do. Which means they thought their house was better than the neighbors', which I thought was ridiculous.

I set a fair price. Then I met with the top real estate man in the area and made him promise to keep the price to himself and potential buyers. I signed the papers on Sunday morning, mentally released it and headed for Newport for a nice, relaxed sail.

I got home at 6 p.m., just as the phone was ringing. It was the real estate agent. He had an offer. He came over at 7:30, and the house was sold at our recommended firm price.

I mention this only because of what happened to the egos in the neighborhood. We vacated in July. Three weeks later the Watts Riots exploded. The beautiful, peaceful Baldwin Hills area became a "tough sell" neighborhood for no good reason at all. Three years later the ego types got maybe 40% less.

As if the move to Downey wasn't exciting enough, 1965 was a bright and shining year because of the Big Ten Club. Sixty-five was my year to be president. After 10 years of being on ice I finally had my shot. It was glorious for several reasons. First Bill Reed, the Big Ten commissioner, suggested that the BTC president attend the annual Skywriters Tour. This is when all the top Midwest sports writers get on a plane in Chicago and in 6½ days visit all 10 campuses plus Notre Dame. They interview all the coaches, and players. It was just a super experience, especially for a sports fan like me.

And '65 was Michigan State's spectacular undefeated season and Rose Bowl visit. As president I was to preside over the BTC Dinner For Champions. A record crowd of 1,300 was packed into the Biltmore Bowl. It was my job to introduce all the Big Ten officials present, including our athletic director Biggie Munn and NCAA Coach of the Year, Duffy Daugherty. Knowing that Woody Hayes, the great Ohio State coach, hadn't made the trip, I told my favorite Woody Hayes story.

"A famous All-American shuffles off his mortal coil and is met at the Pearly Gates by St. Peter. 'Welcome, friend,' says St. Peter. 'Now that you're here, would you like to visit football practice?'

" 'You mean there's a football team up here?'

" 'Certainly. Follow me.'

"So St. Peter takes him from Cloud Nine down to Cloud Six and points to Cloud Five, just below them. There is a gorgeous football field with 100,000 seats, all on the 50 yard line, with football players running up and down the field. On the sidelines is the coach, wearing a short sleeve white shirt, a scarlet and gray tie, and a little black baseball hat with a scarlet and gray 'O' on it. He's ranting and raving and throwing his red telephone all over the place.

"The newcomer says in disbelief, 'Say, isn't that Woody Hayes down there?'

" 'No,' says St. Peter. 'That's God. He just *thinks* he's Woody Hayes.' "

An actor lives for the explosion of sound that rocked the room that moment. I still get goose bumps. Thank you, Woody, wherever you are.

The best of times, sad times, frustrating times and exciting moments. Being so involved in outside activities and trying to figure out what to do now with Speedy gone, I had failed to notice a subtle change in one area—business activity in the No. 1 reason for my being in the Los Angeles area . . . acting. The first sign of the impending change in the industry came from an audition with Bill Melendez. The show: the first Charlie Brown TV special.

Bill had me audition for the voices of the forlorn Charlie Brown, pushy Lucy and one other boy's part. So as not to identify who was reading for what, Bill had us use numbers, not names. When the dust had settled, the creator of the series chose my three numbers. Bill told him who "belonged" to the three numbers. According to Bill, the creator had a fit. He told

Bill, "Under no circumstances will I allow an adult to do these kids' parts. Only kids sound like kids. Audition some more kids!"

He did, and again included my auditions on the tape, this time with different numbers. Again, what's-his-name picked my numbers. Now Bill was in a box. He told his boss the truth. The boss said, "Oh, I was just testing you. I knew it all the time. I really want numbers this, this and this."

So without telling anybody, Bill cast the kids the boss picked but hired me to direct them.

When the next series came up Bill did the same thing and again I won the audition but again the creator refused to use me. He wanted "kids to play kids."

For my acting career it was an ill wind that was sweeping the land. Unfortunately, I didn't know then whether it was just a temporary condition or what. Anyway, it was time to set new goals. But if not acting, what then?

December, 1965. As president of the Big Ten Club of Southern California, Dick presides at the annual BTC Queen's Luncheon. Shown here with the Queen of the 1966 Tournament of Roses, Carole Cota, and J. Randolph Richards, President of the Tournament of Roses Association.

21

The Misfits Win

For the first time since I began setting goals, I was stumped. I just couldn't figure out which way to go. I read every motivational book I could find—all of Emmet Fox's books, Norman Vincent Peale's new book—but I couldn't seem to nail anything down. I was leaning toward business but I still wanted to be a busy actor doing voices on commercials and cartoons. If there's one thing I've learned over the years, *indecision means drifting.* So drift with the flow I did.

With my Alka-Seltzer contract running out, Miles did a nice thing. They weren't sure about Speedy's future so they offered to pick up my option at a slightly reduced salary and release me from the "no compete" clause. I accepted. This gave me some more planning time.

1968 was to be a key year. The free-lance acting business was good but it was changing. More and more young agency directors, Turks as they were called, were insisting that kids do kids' voices. I was doing a lot of work for Mattel toys on their talking dolls and talking games. Hanna Barbera was using me exclusively, sometimes five episodes a day. In another new area, film production companies were hiring me to be on the set to direct the kids.

Strange as it sounds, a Little League team was to be the Angel Voice that indirectly pointed me in a new direction. I applied for a team and was assigned a minor league team. I couldn't make tryouts, which I didn't think was important anyway, so I attended the meeting of team managers where the teams would be determined. When I got there the players' agent handed me a set of twelve 3x5 cards.

"Beals, this is your team. You may call the parents tomorrow and set up a practice. We have the school field reserved at 4 p.m. every day. Take your pick of practice days."

Thinking it strange that my team was already picked for me, I still didn't question it. Then some of my fellow managers wondered if they could see whom I had. Not knowing any of the boys, I showed them the cards.

One said, "Oh, here's a kid that's my boy's best friend, and he lives right next door. Why don't I trade you this kid for our little neighbor boy?"

"Fine, here." The big trade was consummated. This happened with several others. The meeting was concluded, and I went home with my new team. The next day I made calls to the mothers, set up a practice and met the kids at four o'clock on a damp, cold, dreary, March afternoon.

They looked a little bedraggled and not very athletic, but minors are minors, I thought. I also noticed some fathers were there, as usual, hoping against hope just by the way they looked interested they would be picked as an assistant manager. One father brought his son over to introduce him. The kid's older brother was also with him.

"Mr. Beals, this is my boy Billie. He's on your team. He'll never be much of a ball player. Doesn't take to sports much. Takes after his mother. But you're stuck with him, I guess," which was followed by a loud, irritating laugh. Then grabbing his older boy by the shoulder he adds, "This is the athlete in the family. Takes after his old man, huh, Tom?" Tom agreed obediently. "Tom's on the majors. Quite a kid." Then he leaned over to tell me kind of confidentially, but loud enough for all to hear, "Billy, I'm afraid, won't ever amount to much, kinda sickly too. Well, he's all yours. See ya later, son. Have fun."

Kinda gives your heart a real tug, doesn't it. I was in shock. With Billy in tow, my arm around his thin shoulders, I let him help me get the equipment bag out of my car. I rounded up all the kids and sat them down on the bench.

"Fellas, my name is Mr. Beals, and I'm your manager. As of now you are officially the Athletics. The first thing we're going to do is loosen up, then throw a little bit. So grab your gloves and take a slow jog around that tree out there and hustle back. OK. Go."

They even ran funny. One big, tall skinny kid ran as if his ankles were tied together. His mother said he had been a sensational player last year in another town, however, so who was I to judge? While they were running I got out six new baseballs and placed them at 10-foot intervals down the first-base line. Huffing and puffing the kids returned and huddled around me waiting for new orders. "Good. Now I want you six to go stand by the baseballs on the first base line, and you six get out about 30 feet opposite someone with a ball. OK, go." They did. "All right, now you six on the first-base line pick up the ball and, real easy now, throw it to the man opposite you. OK, go."

It was my first hint something was wrong. They all missed. My second hint was some didn't know on which hand the glove was worn. They had them on backwards. I also now had six slightly damp, muddy, new baseballs. "All right, hold it. First go get the baseballs and hold on to them." They did. "Now watch me very closely. Here is how you wear a glove. First of all, how many of you are right-handed?" Talk about shock. Five kids raised their hands. I had seven left-handers on this ball team. I went through proper glove-wearing techniques. "Now, here's how we throw a ball; watch carefully." I picked a kid with a ball, took it, and in slow motion I demonstrated how I wanted it done, ending up throwing it to a kid on the first-base line, right at the target he was holding up. It hit his glove and bounced off.

"Now the boys holding the baseballs throw them to the man opposite you. If it is a bad throw or you drop it, start running around that tree down there. OK, GO!"

In 10 seconds I was all alone. In fact, upon seeing the boys perform, all the fathers were also missing. I was in deep trouble. Throwing practice being a disaster, I switched to hitting and couldn't believe what I saw. Only three kids knew that you held the bat at the small end and hit the ball with the big end. The rest thought you hit it with the knob. The batters—and I went through all 12—had no idea how to hit, or swing the bat or hold the bat, for that matter.

After dinner I thought it out. I decided to go to Ernie Johnson, the most successful high school coach in the area. He got right to the point.

"First key to success is discipline. Give these little kids something to hang their hats on. Make them feel they are something special. A cut above. Show them exactly how to wear their hats and their uniforms and have them shine their baseball shoes, and wear clean shoelaces, tied just so. Assign them a place in the stands, three rows of four each, and have them there at a precise time waiting for you. Assign a very special boy to get the equipment bag out of your car. Make them compete for the honor."

The plan was put into effect immediately. It did set them apart. The other teams were running wild all over the school yard, throwing hats, screaming and yelling. Not the Athletics.

There they sat in the bleachers, four to a row, three rows, with the "bag man" on the lookout for my car.

Ernie then gave me the second key to success. "Fundamentals. Nothing fancy. Solid fundamental baseball. All drills should be fun and no more than 15 minutes in length."

The next step had me set up a parents' meeting at my house. I instructed the parents on how they were to act at the games. I asked them not to coach the kids at home but rather to ask them to demonstrate what they had learned. Then, only applaud the kids, don't yell at them, or me, or the umpires.

Then the final key. "Team unity. Can't win without it. You have big kids, little kids, shy kids, tough kids, weak kids. But somehow you have to get them to know and appreciate one another."

This key was accomplished by asking the mothers to invite another member of the team over for lunch during Easter break. Each boy was asked to write a short report about his visit and something about his teammate. During my phone conversations with the mothers some real shockers turned up.

Every boy on the team had either a severe physiological or psychological problem. These included child abuse, asthma and migraine headaches. Mark, 5'4'', 145 pounds, sucked his thumb and never spoke. "Little" David, youngest of four ball-playing brothers, was not invited to speak at home. The case of two of the boys who seemed out of place was finally cleared up. The boys who had lunch with them both asked, "Mr. Beals, what does retarded mean?" I immediately contacted the parents and confirmed the facts. How they ever got into Little League, I'll never know. I was determined they were going to be baseball players and play in every game.

There wasn't a good student on the team. But somehow I had to make a team out of them. Never in my life had I been so inspired to do so.

That's the cast of characters, and here is how I planned their future in Little League. Win or lose, they were going to be disciplined, polite young gentlemen, knowledgeable about the fundamentals of baseball and about one another. They were also going to know the rules of the game. To accomplish this I got them all rule books and assigned each one a rule to learn and explain to the team—rules such as the balk, stealing, obstruction, interference, asking for time and the 45-foot zone. Fifteen minutes each practice was devoted to this, with results you wouldn't believe.

In our practice games we were the laughingstock of the league. But we were learning to hit, learning to field the ball and making great progress.

The first game I was nervous but tried not to show it. The kids could not have cared less. They didn't know what a game was. They had never played one. Thumb-sucking Mark pitched, Billie caught, and my southpaw infield could be heard chanting, "See the ball, get in front of the ball, pick up the ball and throw the ball." They also hit the ball. A ton. Like 23 runs' worth. Mark pitched a two-hitter, both nubbers to "little David" at third, which he wisely "ate." Mark struck out 12. At the end of the third inning, with six runs in, the bases still loaded, Mark coming up, with two homeruns already slugged, and the opposing pitcher starting to cry, the umpire called the game.

The other team threw gloves, hats, swore loudly. My team mechanically and dutifully ran to them, put their arms around their shoulders and congratulated them, returning to our bench.

They showed no emotion. Why? Because they had never won a game before. They had never won ANYTHING before. Although their parents were going crazy, I had 12 stone-faced kids sitting there waiting for instructions.

"Boys, I am so proud of you. You were just great. You just won your first Little League game."

Eyes brightened, smiles erupted up and down the bench, Billy started applauding, and then they all started clapping. They didn't know why but they did. I shook their hands, and then made the announcement they were waiting for.

"Practice tomorrow four o'clock. Now everyone to the Snack Shack and the snow cones are on me."

They improved with each practice and they kept on winning. We won the first half by winning 10 straight games. By juggling the pitching schedule, I was able to pitch Mark six of the 10 and he won them all. He was batting well over .500 and led the nation in homeruns. Speedy "little David" scored every time he got on first—usually in three pitches or less.

In the second half we won eight straight, lost one, won the last game and ended up in a tie for the second half with the team that beat us. Then I had a problem. I had made long-range plans to go on a flying/golfing vacation to Jekyll Island, Georgia, with my brother, and I had to leave the day after the season was over. I couldn't be with the team for the playoff or the championship game. So I left the team with my assistant manager.

The following Wednesday morning the phone rang in Georgia and it was a telegram from my assistant manager. "You are the proud manager of a championship Little League team. They breezed 23-3. Mark hit two out. No championship game necessary."

But there is more. First some amazing personal victories. David, of course, led all teams in steals. Mark batted .703, led the league in homeruns and was 14-0 pitching. He had one time at bat that proved most memorable.

The opposing pitcher was all elbows and knees and wild but got two quick strikes on Mark. The kids could pick up my voice even with the noise and cheering associated with a ball game. From our bench I said to Mark softly, "Mark, step out and ask for time." He did by gesturing at the umpire; he still hadn't yet spoken. "Mark, he's going to go high and outside with this next one. Understand?" Mark nodded without even looking around. "Keep your eye on it and hit it as hard as you can. I don't care where it goes, but hit it."

We never did find the ball. Our games were played at an elementary school that was 250 feet from home plate. It had air conditioning ducts on the roof. The ball landed on the roof and "one-bounced" the nearest duct.

Billy caught every game and was voted captain. By mid-season his migraines were completely gone. Big David never had one attack of asthma the whole season. "Little" David became the star at home. He knew the rule book better than his four big brothers, and his years of silence at home were ended. In every case, the physiological and psychological problems disappeared. It was amazing what a little self-esteem would do.

Five times during the season the umpires erred in decisions involving both our team and our opponents. Each time, one of my players politely but quickly corrected the umpire, citing section, page and rule . . . verbatim.

During a crucial game we had the bases loaded with two outs and one run down. Our weakest hitter was up, with Mark next. Our kids were really in the game. The opposing pitcher was looking in for his sign when, for some reason, he dropped the ball. Three Athletic runners, two base coaches and seven Athletics on the bench yelled "BALK!" all at the same time. I thought the kid would jump out of his shoes.

Our little batter, all of nine, stepped out of the batter's box and said, "Mr. Umpire, the pitcher balked." And then he closed his eyes as if in deep thought and started quoting the rule, which states in brief that any time a pitcher is on the pitcher's plate or astride the plate and drops the ball it is a balk. The umpire hesitated for just a split second in disbelief, the hitter immediately quoted book, chapter and verse.

The ump started shaking his head no but looked up the rule. As he read it he slowly started shaking his head yes and yelled, "BALK!"

The runner was waved in from third, the pitcher lost his cool and hit the batter on the next pitch. Then Mark came up and settled the whole thing rather quickly by hitting the fence on one bounce.

There is an annual League picnic where all the awards are presented. Only one team, the Athletics, showed up that year. The other teams boycotted it. Word had gotten out the Athletics had garnered all three awards for sportsmanship, the league championship and scholarship. Each proud Athletic went home with three nice trophies.

I was the proudest and most surprised at the Scholarship Award. It meant that these youngsters had shown the greatest improvement in their schoolwork of all kids in the League. It was difficult for me to talk about the team without getting pretty emotional about it. It was surely the "impossible dream."

Yet there was one more gift I alone was to know about. It came after I got home from a Pop Warner football practice. The doorbell rang and there stood Tom and Bill.

"Mr. Beals, could you come out to the car? Our parents would like to speak to you."

I followed them out to the car. Bill's mother did the talking. I could tell there had been tears. Her voice was choked with emotion. "Mr. Beals, we want you to know that Tom and Bill were tested today. And for the first time in their lives they can now attend public school." Then she broke down, crying and smiling. They all were.

The tall, skinny, uncoordinated first basemen were overjoyed; their parents were proud and relieved. It was a joyous scene.

Tom's dad said, "Coach Beals, you'll never know how much we appreciate what you did for these kids." Then he kind of collapsed and broke up. With tears of joy we all shook hands, and they went on their way.

Epilogue . . . a mythical Minor League All-Star team was named. Not a single Athletic made it. My kids had finished first in every statistical category. Usually in Little League you can't vote for your own boys, but all the managers had the final stats. None of the other managers voted my kids. I couldn't understand it. Then the bubble burst.

A manager "accidentally" confessed to an Athletic parent, who immediately confirmed it with the Players Agent, called me and asked if he could come over to the house to see me. He didn't look too pleased as he settled in on the couch.

"You're not going to believe this, Dick. The Athletics were a set-up team. Without you being at tryouts, they knew you wouldn't know one kid from another. So they met privately beforehand and gave you the 12 worst players that tried out."

"But why? What did I do?"

"Your application showed that you were a newcomer to Downey, that you'd coached for ten years at all levels through Pony League and semi-pro, and they wanted to show you up."

I just stared at him.

"In fact, if you will remember the meeting you attended, somehow you had gotten a few players you weren't supposed to get. This manager told me they had to make all kinds of excuses to get some of the kids switched."

"Boy, what a dummy I was. I didn't suspect a thing. How can people be so small over a Little League team? A minor league team to boot."

A while later a bright idea hit me. If those three keys to success—discipline, fundamentals and team unity—would help unsuspecting youngsters, what would it do for those who would knowingly practice these laws? I decided to build a motivational speech around this incredible success story. It was added to my Golden Key list: increased cartoon and commercial voices, new business opportunities and profitable speaking engagement.

THE ATHLETICS
1968 MINOR LEAGUE CHAMPIONS
DOWNEY LITTLE LEAGUE

This team photo was taken prior to the beginning of the season. Litttle did anyone know, especially their manager, that they would win it all: the Minor League championship, the Scholarship trophy and the Sportsmanship trophy.

22
"Angels, Help Me!"

The Wild Blue Yonder beckoned once again. I ventured out to Fullerton Airport one Sunday and began kicking tires. In no time at all I had resoloed and by year's end had my private ticket.

Once cleared for cross-country flying, though, which was in mid-summer, I made many flights to Escondido working on land deals. Through Fio I got to know many fine people.

I mention this only because it was the many flying and driving trips to Escondido that were slowly turning my business head in that direction. I didn't know *what* business, but I was looking. It was also the Escondido Woman's Club that gave me my first "Three Keys to Success" speaking opportunity. Many other speaking engagements followed.

My career as a voice actor was about to take many strange turns. The case was building to look elsewhere for a new career.

Hanna-Barbera had a TV special called Jack and the Beanstalk. It starred Gene Kelly and a new youngster named Bobby Rhia. The kid was cute as a button, could act and dance and supposedly sing. He had five super Sammy Kahn songs to sing, which were recorded. The film was shot in the "blue screen" technique so they could lay HB's finest animation behind it. A rough cut awaited Joe and Bill when they returned from vacation, plus the soundtrack that would be made into an album. They weren't pleased with what they heard . . . .

"What's the matter with you people?" said Bill Hanna. "You can't understand a word the kid is singing. Does he have a speech impediment or what?"

The director responded. "No, Bill, he's growing and his front teeth are, well, I think they call it overbite. He lisps a little."

"A little. Well, we can't live with what we have. Get Dick Beals in here and have him loop it."

"But Joe, it's all shot and animated. Looping would be very expensive and difficult at best."

"Well, let Dick try matching the soundtrack, then. We'll take it from there, but do something."

I had a meeting with the director. They gave me the soundtracks on quarter-inch tape, and the lead sheets and sent me home to practice. When I felt I was ready, we went into a studio and had at it. Using a headset, they plugged the Bobby Rhia track in my left ear and the music track in my right ear. I was required to match his voice and match his timing that I heard in my left ear, correct all his mistakes and record it on the track in my right ear. With the musical director sitting beside me, we ran it and ran it, song by song, until he was satisfied that it was really Bobby singing, but without a speech impediment. It was a long shot, but darned if it didn't work.

The director took the new tracks, transferred them to mag tracks (16-mm film with an audiotape strip in it) and laid them in the sprocket holes. He called Bill down to his basement work area and ran it. Perfect. I was a hero. HB was off and running. But there was a slight problem, which the producer explained over lunch.

"Dick, Bill and Joe are most pleased with what you did. But they have a problem. We can't list your name in the credits as doing the singing."

"Why not, for crying out loud. It's no crime that a kid has an overbite."

"But the kid is a potential star. The network has big plans for him. And if it gets out that he can't sing, everyone gets hurt."

"That's crazy. He can sing, but he has a temporary impediment problem. So big deal." However, it was an offer I couldn't refuse. They paid me well for the work, and I was listed just as a voice for one of the cartoon characters. The morning after the preview showing, to which I was not invited, I got a call from Mrs. Rhia. She was ecstatic and overjoyed.

"Oh, Mr. Beals, how can we thank you enough? You sing beautifully and you sounded just like my Bobby."

"My pleasure, Mrs. Rhia. Bobby has a bright future."

"Oh yes, I know. Already he's being considered for two pictures, several TV specials, and a Broadway show. We're all so proud of him."

My agent called next. "Dick, you're the talk of the town. The secret is out, and people are impressed with what they saw and heard last night."

"Yeah, Charlie, but what can we do about it? How can we capitalize on it?"

"Take out an ad in Variety for the day after the TV showing."

"Saying what?"

"Oh, something like, 'Thanks, Joe and Bill, for the opportunity' and then, 'Dick Beals, singing voice of Jack.'"

Charlie checked it out with HB and they didn't like it, but had no real objections. The show aired and the ad ran the next day. At 9 a.m. my phone rang. It was the once grateful Mrs. Rhia.

"We're going to sue you, Mr. Beals," screamed the stage mother. "How could you do this to Bobby?"

"Do what, Mrs. Rhia? What's wrong with advertising the fact

that I did the singing on Jack and the Beanstalk?'' I think that's called a trap.

"Because we wanted people to think that Bobby did the singing. Now he's ruined. His career is over.'' She was livid.

"Mrs. Rhia, now listen. Bobby's career is not over. He can act, he can dance, but he has a temporary speech impediment caused by an overbite and two very large front baby teeth. June Allyson had the same thing and it didn't hurt her career.'' Actually, it wasn't the same thing, but I was hoping she didn't know this. "Bobby wasn't going to fool anyone with his singing. Anyone listening to him would pick it up instantly. Trust me.''

"No, I won't trust you. We're going to sue you unless you retract the ad and say you didn't do the singing.''

"But who is going to believe that? One phone call to HB and they'll know it's a phony. You're not making sense. No attorney will agree to something as silly as that.''

"No, you're wrong. Our attorney says we have a good case.'' She didn't sound very convincing and she was a lousy bluffer. "We're going to sue you. You just think about that for a while, Mr. Beals.''

"I already have, Mrs. Rhia. No retraction. That's final. That would be dishonest. No deal.''

She hung up. I guess her attorney did, too. I never heard a word. I did report the conversation to Bill Hanna, though. His reaction . . . a low chuckle and a friendly, "Good job, Dick.''

Then two events occurred that shook me right down to the boot straps. My Angels were trying to tell me something.

One was a routine audition. I gave the director all kinds of ideas, different kinds of kids, various ages and personalities, especially young kids, three to five years old. He taped them, of course, to let the client hear them and make a selection. I didn't get the job, I guess, because I heard nothing more about it. Almost nothing.

I was finishing up a session for something and the engineer and I got to talking. He had been the engineer on the other audition. "Ron, who eventually got that job with the little girl's voice in it?''

"You don't want to know.''

"No, really. I'm a big boy now. Who got it?''

"They brought in a four-year-old girl, who could hardly say her own name, put a headset on her, played your tape in her ears, and after three days, they finally got her to mimic your lines. I had to edit bits and pieces of words forever and ever. You could have done it in five minutes.''

"That stinks.''

"Actually your tape still sounded more like a four-year-old

than the four-year-old did. It was rotten. But, that's show biz.''

I was furious. I told my agent about it, but we both knew it was history.

Then the coup de grace. The one stroke that convinced me my livelihood was elsewhere. It was the result of a trip to New York to stand by for a singing assignment for Johnny Whittaker. He was starring in a TV Christmas special and had some super songs. But his singing voice was a bit lacking, and they had me there, secluded in a hotel as insurance, in the event his singing wasn't acceptable. I would then loop it after he left town. Taking advantage of the trip, I contacted 41 TV directors, writers, casting people and other agency types. I told them in letters when I would be in town, that I had a new demo tape for them and I would call them for an appointment first thing Monday morning.

End result: no interviews. Thirty-seven couldn't be reached, nor did they return my calls. Three said to "just leave the tape at the front desk." One sent his secretary out to get it and say hello. It was bitter cold in New York in February of 1969. I was there a week after the gigantic, crippling snowstorm. Trudging around to 41 different offices to drop off tapes was a chore. I was upset, hurt, angry, insulted and everything in between. To try to at least be positive about the whole thing, I remembered why I was there and concentrated on rehearsing the songs for the TV show. Then came the clincher. The phone in my room at the Warwick Hotel rang just after lunch on the third day. It was the producer of the TV show.

"You're excused, Dick. You may go home."

"Go home? I'm here to work. What's going on?"

"The client feels Johnny sings well enough, and he has accepted it. We'd rather you loop it, but they are telling us to the contrary."

I caught a 6:30 flight out of the snow and cold. On the plane ride home I did some serious thinking. Someone was trying to tell me something, and it was about time I listened. Goals had to reassessed. The Golden Key was about to be revised. And the friendly little town of Escondido was beginning to look pretty good. Now, all I had to do was decide if I were willing to take the gamble. Should I open a new business down there? And if so, what? Angel Voices, I'm listening.

23
"As a Small Door Closes . . ."

A year of transition, a year of ups and downs, a year of almost and maybe. As it ran down, there was nothing to hang my hat on. But one experience solidified for me what it was I was looking for. This indirectly caused me to take another big gamble, comparable almost to 1951.

Fred "Curly" Morrison, of Ohio State and Cleveland Browns fame, was a good friend whom I had met through the Big Ten Club. We happened to sit together at a BTC luncheon and got to talking about a new project of his.

"I've formed a company called UV Sports, made a film on jogging with Rocky Marciano, and now we're trying to peddle it."

"Who's your market?"

"We're looking for corporate types that will buy the film and use it internally. We're just starting on that end, though. The film won't be ready for about 10 days. Are you interested in helping us sell it?"

Of course I was. They were super people with whom to work. They kept their end of the bargain and backed me to the hilt. I kept my end of the bargain by contacting people right and left, setting up and making presentations and researching potential clients. With a whole flock of them in Detroit and Chicago, UV Sports sent me back there on a sales trip.

After a while, several factors had been resolved in my mind. There was now absolutely no doubt about it. UV Sports had been the Angel Voice all along. It was telling me what I wanted to know.

First, as hard as I tried, I wasn't able to nail anything down for them. A lot of promises, but no signatures on the dotted line. I had been in the board rooms of the top corporations in the country—Ford, Sears, Prudential, Polaroid. I made my pitch, but couldn't get the order. Still, I got there.

Second, I loved putting on a coat and tie and being in an office every day. I loved the daily challenge of having to sell myself in a letter or on the phone and then following through with the presentation and the sales pitch.

Third, I now knew that I wanted my own business, selling my own product or service, in my own office. What I had been fighting all these months, was making another move and taking another major gamble, and giving up the acting business after 18 challenging years. The Angel Voices were trying to tell me it was time to move on.

A trip to Escondido just about brought my decision. Fio set up a coffee meeting with some of the top movers and shakers in town. By this time, they all knew me and my background. It was one of the stockbrokers who served as the top Angel.

"Heck, Dick, your business is marketing and advertising and selling. Why not open up your own ad agency down here?"

Yeahs, and sures, and why nots were heard all around the table.

"What kind of competition is there?"

"Oh, a fellow named Jack Petersen is just out from New York, and mostly retired, but he has a one-man operation going. Another man has a small office with a couple named Jim and Melba Cotton with him. They're doing pretty good, but rumor has it that they're thinking of splitting off on their own."

Fio then jumped in quickly, "Looks as if this is the time to make your move."

The feature writer for the local paper popped in with, "Wouldn't that make a good story. Seems as if you have a city waiting for you, Dick."

The meeting broke up, and I was deep in thought walking back to Fio's office. Clearing his throat noisily, Fio broke the silence. "I'll lend you an office today. Why not call Jack Petersen and Jim Cotton and get a feel for the area?"

So I did. It was amazing the different reactions. Jack and I had many mutual friends in the New York area, and he was all positive and encouraging. "Why not, always room for one more. I've got some account ideas for you to get started on. Let me know when you're going to make the move. We'll have lunch."

I couldn't reach Jim Cotton, but someone in Fio's office did, later. Cotton was negative. "Not much business here anyway, but there certainly is no room for another agency. He's wasting his time."

Now, why did he have to say that? That was a downright challenge in my book.

I had had enough of the acting business, the L.A. freeways, the smog. I wanted something new. Over Christmas I finalized my plans. I decided to wrap things up in January and leave my parents in the Downey house until I got a feel for business in Escondido.

On January 21, 1970, the movers came in for my office furniture, and I was off to Escondido, California.

24

Hit the Ground . . . Knocking

Compared to the pace of Los Angeles, Escondido was like putting on a pair of slippers at the end of the day. Yet it meant starting a new business from scratch, and it was evident from the outset it would involve a lot of scratching.

My approach to this new challenge was utilizing The Golden Key again. I wrote down all those things for which I was grateful. My list began with my health, my furnished duplex, my office, my safe car, my family, a few other things, and then I added my three new desires, as if they had already been granted to me.

"Thank you, God, for my new accounts. Thank you, God, for my new permanent residence. Thank you, God, for my many new friends. I reminded myself of the Golden Key law. Because I'd thought of these new desires, it meant that they were already in existence. So, I gave thanks for receiving them. Now, it was time for the Angels to go to work, with me right behind them.

My approach was to study the local newspaper and see who advertised. If I thought I could improve on their ads, then go after them. Then, take a look at those businesses in town that didn't, and find out why not.

The Times Advocate did one more thing that helped launch my new advertising agency. They assigned a reporter to interview me, and two days later, photo spread and all, a sizable feature story appeared. Just like that, I was a Hollywood celebrity in Escondido. I was also the only ad agency that was on the streets knocking on doors when businesses opened in the morning. And the knocking continued until closing time. It was Hollywood all over again. It worked 18 years earlier. There was no reason why the same THINK BIG philosophy wouldn't continue working it's magic.

Coach John McKay, of the USC Trojans, had a saying that inspired me to action each day. The saying came out of a win over Stanford at the Coliseum one Saturday. It was not just *a* win, it was the 10th straight win over the John-Ralston-coached team.

With reporters crowded around him, Ralston complained, "USC was lucky, just plain lucky."

Hearing that, the reporters ran down the tunnel to Coach John McKay, and repeated Ralston's quote. McKay smiled, flicked the ash off his cigar and mused, "You tell Coach Ralston, that luck takes over *after* you have given 110%."

That was my approach to the new advertising challenge in Escondido. It was the positive approach, full time, with all the energy I could muster on the job each day. If it was worth doing, it was worth doing right.

First, I attacked the two mavericks—the biggest auto dealer and a sizable furniture account. I came up with some ideas they liked and they gave me a shot. Then a candidate for mayor in a neighboring town, a chiropractor, a mobile home park, and the local country club, where my house was being built.

Growing pains developed sooner than I expected. I needed a good art director, someone who could whip out layouts, spec type, giving me more time to be calling on new accounts. I put out the word at the newspaper, hoping that one of their artists might want to moonlight, but no one volunteered. I also knew that I couldn't truly afford to hire anyone full time or provide office space.

Two days later, the Angels delivered. There was a quiet knock on my office door, and in walked a rather shy, smiling, heavy-set man, middle sixties maybe, huffing and puffing from walking up the stairs.

"Mr. Beals, do you have a few minutes?" he said, choking a little and perspiring a lot.

"Certainly, come on in."

I got up from my desk and motioned him to sit on the couch. As he plunked down heavily onto the couch, he was giving me and everything the once-over as quickly as possible, especially my art table, hoping I wasn't noticing.

"Nice office. Is it new?"

"Yes, just opened up last month. Only office space in town, actually."

"Well, let me get to the point. I know you're probably busy. My name's Ed Estep. I moved here from New Jersey with my family. I don't know what kind of ad agency you have here, but my real estate man, Don Kidd, suggested I call on you."

"Sure, I know Don Kidd."

"Well, I was the art director in an ad agency for 30 years, retired out here now, but I'd kind of like to keep my hand in. Do you need any help?"

And that was that. He preferred to work out of his home, on a job-by-job basis, at a reasonable hourly rate.

If it's right for me, it's right for everybody, as the man said. I was quick to find out that Ed Estep was right for me, and he was happy as could be.

Business moved ahead at a rapid pace. With Ed's layouts and counsel, we were producing solid ads that were producing increased sales for my new clients.

Even San Diego radio station reps started calling on me, in hopes of selling my clients on radio. One in particular, Mark McKinney, brought about another important change in my business. I had never really gotten to know one of my competitors in town, Jim Cotton. He and his wife had a small but successful agency, with some pretty good-sized accounts, including some key industrial accounts. I had talked to a few of them, but found that Cotton was pretty well entrenched.

Mark was a true Angel Voice, whether he knew it or not. At my request, he arranged a luncheon to introduce the two adversaries.

When Cotton arrived, a few minutes late, I sensed he was uncomfortable, a bit shakey, yet trying to appear bored with the whole thing.

Everything but business was discussed. Our host, after our food was served, finally tried to break the ice. "Dick is doing a pretty good job with some top retail accounts in town."

Cotton half smiled, and said, "Well, he can have them. They don't spend any money. I have all the top industial accounts in town. They have the budgets worth going after."

Mark looked at me kind of funny, waiting for my reaction. I didn't even look up from my salad. Finishing a bite I said, quietly, "Well, I do the best I can with what I have to work with." But Mr. Cotton had said the wrong thing at the right time. I'd seen a gauntlet thrown before, and I'm sure he didn't mean it as such, but he said it to the wrong, hungry ad man.

The next day, from the Chamber of Commerce, I had the list of all industrial accounts in town, and the door knocking began. Bit by bit, with Ed Estep helping me, we nailed down one account after another. Then another miracle happened.

Cotton was bought out by a San Diego agency that was trying to get a foothold in the north San Diego county area, in the center of which was Escondido. I didn't like the sound of this, but it didn't deter my positive, all-out approach, day after day. In fact, it cranked it up a bit. About that same time, I was asked to join the Rotary Club. Seemingly two unrelated events, but not when you believe in Angel Voices.

Ed Estep was gradually running out of gas, with all the work I was giving him, and was hinting around that he might not be able to help me quite as much. But the Angels were way ahead of me. Another highly skilled, unemployed industrial artist, from the Quad cities area in Iowa called on me, and showed me a heck of a portfolio. He too wanted to work out of his home. We agreed on a reasonable hourly rate, and we were in business. It was perfect for everyone—well, almost everyone.

In time, Cotton's new San Diego outfit lost interest in his

Escondido accounts. Then Cotton's boss got into an argument with the biggest account in town, Formulabs, the vice president of which, Jack Raymond, was a friend of mine in Rotary. Before the afternoon was out, Formulabs had switched agencies.

Business continued to improve, necessitating a move into new, larger offices. Despite the rapid growth, the Golden Key always had that prayerful request added to it, "New major accounts, and a larger, more profitable ad agency." And the Angels never failed me. This time though, with the strangest twist yet. The Angel this time was my new client, Jack Raymond. We were wrapping up a meeting when he suddenly changed the subject.

"Are you ready for a real shocker?" he began, impish grin and all.

"If it's good news, yes."

"Your old pal, Jim Cotton, is unhappy down in San Diego and would like to relocate in Escondido."

"Doing what?"

"As an account exec and writer in an ad agency."

"Surely you jest. There's only one game in town, and I don't need an account exec, unless he can bring me in a bunch of huge accounts to pay his way."

"How about the McKeon and the Dixieline accounts?"

"But he can't get those. They belong to his new outfit. They'd never let them go."

"Wanna bet?"

"You're kidding."

"Expect a call from Cotton."

Cotton called. We had a meeting. The new accounts in his pockets were sizable, and he assured me that they would follow him to his new company.

The move meant a big boost in profits, despite the additional below-the-line costs. But the instability of the man was a concern. So I decided to sit on it a while, and turn it over to a higher power. "Let go, and let God," is the way I turned things over. For me, the tough part is letting go completely. I guess that's a common problem for everyone. I knew from experience I had to turn it over 100% if I wanted positive results. I had to get *me* out of the way. So I did. The answer came a few days later. As I awoke one morning, I heard a voice, from out of nowhere, crystal clear, saying, "It's right for everyone!"

I suddenly had a new account executive, a good creative writer, an experienced public relations man, three new major accounts and a larger, more profitable ad agency.

143

25
9161Q

Dick Beals & Associates grew rapidly. We were doing good work. Going after every account that moved had its pitfalls, sometimes, but overall we were growing steadily.

If there was a weakness in the organization, it was my management skills. From my acting background, I expected everyone to give 100% to the team, no questions asked. I had never had to deal with personality conflicts or poor work habits. Into the third year, it was obvious that the creative director, though multitalented, was not doing his share of the creative work. A fine watercolor artist, he had a studio on the side, which his wife operated. I wasn't aware that he was taking company time to supply his studio with paintings.

Cotton complained constantly, but I was slow to take action. Cotton, on the other hand, would bring in accounts, assuring me they had agreed to the proposed budget. But billing and collecting are two different things. Cotton was only interested in the billing and being able to work the account. I was having a difficult time with some of the collectibles.

So these were the conditions I found myself facing. It took a trip back to Birmingham, Michigan, to attend my 30th high school class reunion to think things over, get fresh opinions and make some decisions.

A family friend of many years was the Angel Voice that I was looking for. She said, "It is wrong to hold on to people against their will."

I argued, "Yes, but this man would be crushed if he was released."

"Maybe, at first, but down deep he knows he is not in his right place. It might be the pressure. He might be burned out."

"Now, there's a point that I hadn't thought of. Lately, he's been bringing in other artists and having them make presentations, for work on our accounts."

"And what did you say to that?"

"No, of course. I only want to pay one creative director's salary."

"Dick, you'd be doing him a favor. Let him go. Give him his freedom. Some day he will thank you for it."

I returned to the office on Monday morning, early. First item of business was a meeting with the creative director. "D.R., I've decided to make a change. I'm giving you two weeks notice, effective this date."

Shock and a blank expression replaced the smile. "But why?"

"You are taking off too much time. You are not being honest with me. You tell everyone you are going over to the printer, when in fact you are going out painting. You are not functioning as a creative director should."

"Is it because Cotton was complaining all the time?"

"No. I listened to him, but decided to check on things myself. This is my decision, alone. You are the first to hear about it."

"OK, but I want some vacation time, too."

"No, none at all. I said two weeks notice. Under the circumstances, that is generous. Your so-called visits to various suppliers will be charged as vacation time."

He hung his head for a moment, got up, headed back to his office, got his keys, rushed out the door with a, "See you around, folks," and that was that.

When Cotton and the art director got in, I buzzed them, had a quick meeting and made the announcement. The art director, who had worked for D.R. in Iowa, was speechless. Jim Cotton flushed and only stammered a bit.

"Jim, you are now creative director, and Len, you will be working directly with Jim. He will need all your creative juices, so go to it."

As they left my office, I wondered what they must be thinking. Then I happened to glance at my phone, and I noticed a lot of the lines were in use. It wasn't 8:15 a.m. yet, and I was worn out. I spent the rest of the morning calling a few key clients and explained my move. No problems there.

The big shock came about two months later. It was late, and I was about to head on home when Jim Cotton came in, sat down hurriedly, and blurted out what must have been his carefully rehearsed speech. "I've been offered a job with a major retail store, and I have to take it."

Why I smiled and then chuckled, I'll never know, but I did. I guess it was his rehearsed delivery, or how uncomfortable he looked, but whatever it was, it was the one reaction he didn't expect.

"A major retail store? Doing what?"

"Doing undercover work. We try to find out the sources of internal shrinkage, and report it to management."

"I wish you well, of course, but I sure thought you were happy here. How about McKeon and Dixieline, do they know?"

He squirmed a bit, looked at his feet, crossed and uncrossed his legs, and looking out the window, said, "No, I'll talk to them tomorrow."

He was a bad actor. I thought, "He knows something."

In a few weeks, he departed. Two days after that, the new

McKeon manager for San Diego County, a fellow Michigan Stater, dropped in to review his ad campaign and virtually canceled the whole thing. The Dixieline vice president called me the same day and cut back everything to the nub. It was time to regroup.

If there was ever a time to test my faith in Divine Guidance, this was it. It was certainly a time to rethink my long-term goals and objectives. Knowing that prayers are always answered, I had a hard time accepting that this new situation was subconsciously what I wanted. But the thought kept popping back, if it's right for everyone else, it's right for me. So, I figured the smaller door had closed and a bigger door had already opened, somewhere. I told myself to get back up on my horse and head for the larger door.

First, I sat down with those in the firm who would most likely be concerned. I assured them nothing would change, their jobs were secure, we were financially sound, and new accounts would be found to keep us busy and profitable.

Then I took stock of just exactly where I was headed and where I wanted to be in one year, five years, ten years. First on my list was: 1. New accounts that fit the talents of the existing staff. (This meant creative writing I could handle and layouts the art director could handle.) 2. Involvement in the community. 3. New business that would involve flying. 4. My own airplane.

Five years out, my plan was a bit hazy, but in my mind's eye it went something like this. I wanted to be a part of a larger agency that could handle all the creative and production side of the business, allowing me more time to fly, speak, and go after new business. The association would still allow me to be independent, with my own company, to do with what I wished.

My first phone call went to my tried-and-true mentor, Forrest Owen, now senior executive VP with BBDO, headquartered in Minneapolis. As usual he gave me sound advice.

"You're OK. You can handle whatever comes along. Don't give it another thought."

"Yeah, but these guys will be tough to replace."

"Don't replace them. You do it. If they weren't doing the job, and they weren't a part of the team, then it was just a matter of time, anyway. Good riddance."

"OK. Any other thoughts?"

"Yes. Ad Age has seminars several times a year, in Chicago. They are extremely well done. Find out about them and attend them."

As usual, the man's advice was right on the money. I did attend their seminars. I learned a ton, especially from the other small agency executives in attendance. With my new confident attitude, things began to pop at the office.

My approach was to start scratching again. From the San Diego Chamber of Commerce I obtained a list of businesses. From that list, which I refined even further, I settled on our prospect list, and the calling began.

The results were mind-boggling. New accounts were coming in at a miraculous rate. And they were all the type of accounts we wanted. Accounts that required nuts-and-bolts type copy, the kind I could handle. "When a small door closes, a larger door has *already* opened."

Every day, I continued to review my Golden Key list. Community involvement was next, but I hadn't a clue of what that might be. As in the past, it found me, sooner than I expected. It was at Rotary, and I was at the head table to discuss the Rose Bowl game. To my right was my client, Jack Raymond. To my left was a fellow Spartan, Jim Slezak, superintendent of the elementary school district. Both are well over six feet tall. Their conversation drifted to the upcoming school board election and took place across the top of my head. I was eating, and thinking about my upcoming contribution to the luncheon.

"Anyone running yet, Jim?" asked Jack, a past president of the school board.

"Just Merle Aleshire, the incumbent, and a couple of concerned mother types."

"When is the deadline?"

"January 4."

"Any ideas?"

"I got one."

"Who?"

I was then aware of dead silence.

"Really?" said Jim.

"Ask him," said Jack.

"You ask him," said Jim.

Then, with Jack's typical sense of humor, he reached over and tapped my left shoulder, as Jim reached across and tapped my right shoulder. I snapped my head one way, then the other, and saw two very large gentlemen staring at me, with big smiles.

"Hey pal, we just volunteered you. Congratulations," said Jack.

"For what?" The drift of their conversation pieced itself together in my mind. "Who me? School board? Are you crazy?"

Then the sales pitch began in earnest. They would help me. Jim would bring me up to speed on current events. Jack would help raise money for my campaign. They would both help me with campaign literature. I was an instant candidate.

I was only moderately interested until a chance remark by a school board trustee. He was a rather sizable young man, 6'4", 250, a phone company employee, not much in the way of an education, and little, if any tact. We were at a photo session to promote a YMCA fund-raising drive, of which I was chairman. This was Raymond's idea, designed to get me added visibility. While we were waiting for the photographer to get there, the trustee said, "I hear you're running for our board."

"Yes, that's right. I felt it was time to give something back to the community."

"I was kind of surprised to hear that."

"Why?"

"Well, most people associate size with intelligence."

Thud. Looking at this big clod, and usually not being at a loss for a quick retort, I swallowed my immediate thought and answered with a smile, "Well, what you see, is what you get." And walked away. But, oh, was I ticked, and was I determined to win one of the two seats open on the board.

And I did. Only the incumbent edged me, in total votes. The other 16 candidates bit the dust.

Quite by accident, I got my revenge on my oversized fellow trustee. We were in a meeting and had just been presented with an autographed softball by someone grateful that we had supplied their league with a place to play.

She tossed me the ball from the audience, which I deftly caught and proceeded to examine. Mr. Clod said sarcastically, from the other end of the conference table, and with great authority, "Well, don't hog it, let me see it too."

Believe me, it was unintentional, but while still smiling at the person in the audience, I flipped the ball, backhanded, catching the unsuspecting Clod on the very tip of his big nose. The crowd erupted in laughter, then fell silent, when they realized he was really hurt. Being the big brave racquetball player that he was, he shook it off. That was the last time I heard any derogatory remark from El Cloddo.

My Golden Key request for, "Business that would involve flying," happened, like everything else, quickly and like magic. I had worked my way up to Bonanzas, the top of the line in aircraft. I was renting used Bonanzas at a San Diego area airport, but like all pilots, I always wanted to fly newer models. In a rapid series of events, a Beech salesman asked me if I wanted a demonstration in a new Bonanza. I flew both of us out to El Centro for lunch, and he demonstrated the finer points of this gorgeous airplane.

The price was out of my range, but I asked him if he knew

148

of anyplace where I could rent a new one. I knew this was impossible, but by now I should know better. He gave me the name of a man in Los Angeles who was thinking of buying a fleet of them and intended to place one at Montgomery Field, for rental income.

The man, Dick Kress, met me at Palomar Airport for lunch. He not only wanted to rent me his new airplanes, but needed an advertising agency to help him promote his new campaign. Now, that's magic.

We helped him promote a charter business, using the Bonanzas. We even got him the name, Bonanza Airlines, which had suddenly been abandoned by the previous airline company.

For over a year I had new Bonanzas to fly. He even flew me back to Wichita to the Beech factory to pick up new planes, have my picture taken for our publicity campaign, and fly those new babies back.

Into the second year, he overextended a bit, had to discontinue the advertising, take the airplane back to Los Angeles, and my dream world was over. At least, so I thought. By now, I should have remembered that, ''When a smaller door closes . . . .''

Something happened that would convince me forever that, ''Turning your requests over to a higher power,'' really works. If I was going to fly now that speaking engagements and new business were taking me to faraway places, then I wanted a Bonanza, an F33A, the model with a straight tail, not the ''V'' tail. I knew exactly the equipment I wanted on it. This included electric trim, a button on the yoke that controlled the elevator trim. Without that, it was quite a reach for me to operate it manually.

Dollarwise, a '70-'71 model was within range. I was warned though, by experts, that I wouldn't find electric trim on a Bonanza until their '74 model, and kits were expensive. Trim or no trim, it was a major expenditure, but I was just about ready. The dollars were there, but I just couldn't seem to part with them. I worried this thing into the ground. Then, one Sunday morning after looking through the L.A. Times for the hundredth time, and not finding any Bonanzas, I got a legal pad, a pencil, and tried to figure out my next move.

Something told me to write down all the positive statements I could think of. 1. The money is there. 2. I have a business need for an airplane. 3. It is safer to maintain and fly my own airplane. 4. The perfect airplane will be there at the perfect time, with just the right equipment. 5. God knows what I need, when I need it, and it will be perfect for everyone. So let this thing go, and let God take charge. Who am I, trying to do His job?

The weight that lifted off my shoulders was incredible. I literally forgot all about it, and went about my chores on that particular Sunday. That same evening, I found myself glancing through that same L.A. Times section again. Why I looked into the F column, instead of B for Bonanza column, I'll never know. But there, popping out at me, an ad read: "F33A Bonanza, '71 model, 400 hours Total Time, IFR equipped, new Annual, $48,500. Call—," and the phone number, in the San Jose area.

The price was the hang-up. It was high. The next morning, I called the number, got all the information, and told the man I'd get back. Then I called Bill Williams, general manager of a Cessna dealership owned by a close friend, and a fellow pilot in Rotary. I had been pestering him for months, until he told me to stop until I had the money and the commitment to buy an airplane.

"Bill, I think I've found the airplane."

"Again?"

"It sounds perfect, except for the electric trim, and I think the price is a bit high."

"Give me the info."

I did. "I talked to him, but didn't talk money."

"OK, here we go again," he said, with a big sigh. "If the price is right, and the airplane is right, is it a go?"

"Yes."

"The price. If I can save you, say, $3,500, can I make a deal?"

"If you agree that's fair, then it's a go."

"I know this guy. Let me see what he says. Sit tight." Forty-five minutes later Bill Williams was on the phone. "It sounds good. He agreed on the money, mainly because I have a Baron here that he needs, and we swung a deal. It is being flown down today. My people will check it over top to bottom. If it is 'as is,' I will fly it down so you can fly it, probably tomorrow afternoon."

"Good work, Bill. Give it the once-over and call me."

Bill flew the plane down to Palomar the next day. It was a beauty. When the prop stopped turning, I climbed up onto the wing with my flight bag, forgetting they had to get out. I wasn't excited!

After they got out, I put my cushions into place, put on my "feet," the man who brought it down from San Jose got in the back, and Bill eased into the front. I was stunned. It was perfect. Then as my hand was holding onto the yoke, I felt my thumb hit something I wasn't expecting. It was the electric trim button.

I turned to the pilot in the back seat and snapped loudly,

"Why didn't you tell me it had electric trim?"

Almost in shock, eyes like saucers, he said, "I didn't think it was important."

Bonanza 9161Q was mine. Thank you, God.

Dick with his first airplane, Bonanza 9161Q. He had just finished a cross country flight to Nut Tree airport, Vacaville, California.

Dick in 9161Q, reading back his instrument clearance to Burbank Airport, in the Los Angeles area. He is heading for a recording session at Hanna-Barbera. The two hour, 15 minute drive is but a 28 minute flight in his Bonanza.

26
Flying, Speaking and Sammy Davis, Jr.

Owning an airplane was the catalyst to acquiring new business and finding a new profession.

It started with being asked to give talks at nearby Rotary Clubs. Rotarians, visiting from other clubs, told their program chairmen, and suddenly, I was in demand. The Rotary district governor placed me on his speakers bureau list, one that went to over 35 clubs in San Diego County. Other districts also got that list, so I was a hot prospect. My fee was willingly paid.

My presentations always mentioned the magic words, advertising and marketing, although my talks were motivational, one centered around that Little League team in Downey. I had another entitled, The TV Commercial, Why and How. In the introduction, and in the context of the talk, my business was mentioned. Bit by bit, I began picking up new accounts in outlying areas which could only be serviced by having an airplane.

Then another perfect event took place. The caller said he was from Wells, Rich, Greene, the ad agency in New York that handled the Alka-Seltzer account. Yes, Alka-Seltzer was still going strong.

"Yes, sir, good morning, what can I do for you?"

"Is this Dick Beals?"

"Yes, it is, sir."

"Are you the voice of Speedy Alka-Seltzer?"

"Yes, sir, the one and only."

"Would you be interested in doing a spot for us?"

"Of course," I said, trying to hide my absolute glee.

"Well, I'll be darned. I finally found you."

"Yes, you did, sir, alive and well. When is this blessed event to take place?"

He set a date in New York, we agreed on the money, and Speedy came alive again to help Miles Labs celebrate this country's bicentennial.

A seed had been planted, though. I found I had missed the business. The challenge of doing a good, effective commercial lit the old fires somewhere inside. On the flight home, I did some planning and dreaming, but with no new voice-over business in sight, I let it slide, and my thoughts returned to Escondido, the ad agency and my speaking prospects.

Soon enough, things began to happen. A Big Ten Club friend, Carl Rogers, was chairman of a Rotary district conference in

Palm Springs. He retained me to give a talk there. Also speaking was Jim Tunney, the NFL referee. Jim encouraged me to join the National Speakers Association. At his recommendation, I flew 61Q to Louisville to attend their national convention. There I got a feel for what speakers were charging, how they were advertising their wares and getting more engagements.

It was in Louisville, at Bowman Field, that I also learned again even the pros had a hard time accepting that someone 4'6" could fly a sophisticated airplane. I was headed for Dallas, for a business meeting. The weather around Louisville was overcast, threat of rain, thunderstorms. While preflighting I noticed the usual binoculars popping up in the tower. I was under their closest scrutiny. I waved, they waved, and that was all. I filed my IFR flight plan, got into my airplane, cranked it up and contacted the tower.

"Bowman Tower, Bonanza niner-one-six-one-Quebec, ready to taxi, instruments to Dallas."

Long pause, then, "Uh, Bonanza niner-one-six-one-Quebec, uh, you're not going to fly that alone, are you?"

A few humorous quips flashed into my mind, but I just answered with a grin, "Yes, sir, just little old me."

They even went so far as to try to catch me on procedures, such as the clearance read-back, complicated taxi instructions, another clearance read-back, to no avail. Sensing what they were doing, I stuck right to the book. I guess I passed their test. As I headed up into the soup, they transferred me to Louisville Departure Control, with a friendly, "Have a nice trip, sir," and I was on my way.

Quite suddenly back home, some of my accounts mushroomed, especially Formulabs. Another client asked me to help him set up a sales team. I was faced with more business, some I could not handle myself. I needed creative advertising and someone to handle the advertising production. I knew from experience I couldn't buy one without the other. This would mean eliminating my art director and most of my office staff. And this was a seemingly impossible task. Of course, I should have known better than to think that. "When one door closes . . . ."

"A Mr. Manning, on line one," said my secretary.

"Who?"

"Mr. Don Manning. He said he met you at an SDAAA meeting."

"Yes, I remember. Thank you." I punched the blinking button. "Don Manning, good morning."

Don Manning had a successful industrial advertising agency

in San Diego. I didn't have a clue as to why he was calling me. After some small talk, his tone turned serious.

"Hey Dick, how about lunch one of these days?"

"Sure. What's up?"

"Well, maybe it's time for you to see what we're doing, and see if we can't do some things together."

"Like what?"

"Well, I'm looking for ways to keep my art staff busy and maybe I can help you on the creative side. And, frankly, there are new accounts out there we could get if we pitched them together."

Just like that, the larger door opened.

We agreed to try out the relationship on a Formulabs project. It was obvious from the start Don Manning was a pro, ethical and efficient. We were off and running.

In no time at all, I had three businesses going at once, the ad agency, nationwide speaking engagements, a new marketing company and a sales organization to develop. And all of them involved the use of my airplane. As if that wasn't enough, I was now president of the Escondido Elementary School Board and on the board of directors of the Escondido Rotary Club. I was up at 5, into the office by 7, home around 7, and telling myself how much fun I was having being busy and finding new challenges.

It was soon a lesson in balancing time. My Golden Key changed a bit, though. I prayed for guidance, new business contacts, effective salespeople and proper business direction. It was simply astounding, no, miraculous, how these prayers were answered.

One by one, my new business ventures developed into what was best for everyone, but in ways unlike those I had forecast.

Manning and I took off like gangbusters. Formulabs, with Don's creative skills, was soon showing large profits, and so was I.

No matter what we did for Formulabs, it worked. And I give Don Manning all the credit. I wrote the nuts-and-bolts copy, but his genius designed the ads. The same could be said for all my other accounts and the new ones we cultivated.

In six months, I had my client's new sales organization in place. The speaking business was a treat. Somehow I got on a mailing list of corporations seeking motivational speakers. This was rewarding work, being able to pass on the philosophy that worked so well for me.

The next step was to take some time and plan ahead. I knew the Golden Key worked. I also knew that if I wanted my dreams to come true, all I had to do was dream them. All kinds of things

With Don Manning, standing, and Art Director Dave Dawson, Dick reviews a layout for one of their advertising clients.

Nancy Sundeen, of Manning and Associates, demonstrates her computer magic as they review copy and typesetting possibilities on a client's layout. Nancy was a Rose Parade Princess in 1968.

were placed on my list of possibilities. Did I truly like the advertising business and my association with Manning and Associates? How about getting back into the voice-over business again? How about more speaking opportunities? I still loved to coach young people, especially football and baseball. How about that? The school board election was coming up. Did I enjoy that type of community service? Instead of making up my list this time, I pondered all these options and prayed for guidance.

Then, one day I found myself making out my list. I don't remember picking up the paper or the pencil. I was just suddenly aware of making out a list.

1. A successful advertising business, with a limited but quality client list.
2. Voice-over work.
3. Coach young people, on a limited basis, time permitting.

A week later, one lovely, bright, sunny July morning, my phone rang.

"This is Dick Beals."

"Is this Dick Beals who used to do the voice of Speedy Alka-Seltzer?"

"Yes, it is."

"I'm Margaret Cancassi, with Wells, Rich, Greene, in New York. We'd like you to come back and do some Speedy spots for us. You'll be working with Sammy Davis, Jr. Are you available?"

"Certainly. When?"

She gave me the date and the particulars. Then added, "This is scale thing, of course. No big deal."

"My dear, an Alka-Seltzer commercial is serious business. I am not a scale actor. I've been Speedy for 27 years. But I'll make a deal with you."

"Yes?"

"If Sammy does it for scale, so will I."

"Sammy Davis doesn't do anything for scale."

"Right. Neither do I."

"Well, I'll have to have our business manager talk to you about this."

"Excellent. I'll be here."

The business manager balked, too, but 10 minutes later he called back with full approval.

The spots were for the 1980 Winter Olympics. They sent me lead sheets and music tracks in advance, which was helpful.

Working with Mr. Davis was an experience. Margaret Cancassi warned me he might be difficult.

"He likes to walk in, do one or two takes and go home."

"Margaret, there isn't a voice actor in the world that can do that. Be aware that I'll probably need 10 takes to get the

155

performance I want. Miles deserves the very best, and that's what they are going to get.''

We arrived early, of course, and I used the time to get warmed up and rehearse the spots. Then the man himself made his entrance. The coterie consisted of a manager, his secretary, Sammy's secretary, his bodyguard, a messenger type and an account executive from the agency. I was introduced to Sammy, but he barely acknowledged my presence.

We rehearsed the material at the console in the control room, then adjourned to the studio. For his size, his voice was powerful. He *was* a quick study and his knowledge of music was incredible.

I decided I would determine when we had a satisfactory take, whether he liked it or not. In advance, I asked the director to listen for areas where I might slip out of Speedy's character. I knew from my rehearsals at home where I was having problems.

Sammy's volume was overpowering in some places, causing me a problem. I brought that up, but Sammy disagreed. I asked for a playback, and reluctantly, he agreed and changed his approach. After the 10th take, I was satisfied and so was the director. We moved on. Standing in the back of the control room I spotted Miss Cancassi. Her big wink was all I had to see.

The second spot was even better. We were both warmed up and our voices were blending better and better.

The spots had to be tested by the agency first. If they were graded high enough, we were to do two more for the summer Olympics. The testing showed Speedy and Sammy were a hit. Five weeks later, Margaret Cancassi was back on the phone, and we set another session.

These spots were more difficult. The music was a Russian theme, played by a balalaika, at a rapid tempo. The lyrics included the tongue-twisting phrase, ''Plopski, plopski, fizzski, fizzski, oh what a relief it is-ski!''

When I got to the studio I was informed Sammy would arrive later. ''He said he preferred to work alone.'' My 10-take approach wasn't appreciated. So I worked with the writer at the piano until he was satisfied, then we went at it. It was a tough session. The music went so fast that the lyrics were barely understandable. Eventually, the director was pleased, I was excused and I got ready to leave. In walked Sammy, with only his bodyguard and secretary.

I decided to stay for a while. I wanted to see if Sammy could master these spots, superstar as he was. His bodyguard somehow knew I had a plane, so we sat in the corner talking airplanes. Suddenly, I was aware of a heated discussion going on between the director and Sammy.

"What do you mean you can't sing these lyrics? You've had them for two weeks. You're just finding out now you can't sing them?"

Sammy looked into the control room, spotted me, and looked for just a second like he wished I wasn't there.

"I can't sing these lyrics." He paused, thought carefully about his next statement, then blurted it out. "There are certain words and phrases I can't handle."

The director now looked at me, looked at the agency rep, thought a minute, then pushed the button and said, "OK, let's get what we can. Take it from the top. Give it to me the best you can and we'll do something."

I decided it was best to depart before they got rolling again, got permission to leave, and I went back to my hotel.

It was around 1 a.m., Monday Night Football was just about over, when my phone rang. It was Margaret Cancassi.

"Dick, can you come back here? We've got a problem."

"Certainly, I'll be right there."

The director wasted few words. "Sammy couldn't give us much we could use. You're going to have to do it all again, in the clear, and cover for Sammy. We're in a bind, because tomorrow at 10 a.m., they are on the set shooting this. With Sammy's schedule we can't delay it one hour."

Some of Sammy's lyrics were tough, but after a few takes, and excellent direction, they bought it. I was excused. I was also invited to be on the set in the morning.

Sammy didn't have much to say to me; in fact, not a word. My old pal from Miles, Mitch Streicker, did though.

"I understand you saved our neck early this morning?"

"You have a good team working on these spots, Mitch. They knew just what they wanted. If I helped them out, then fine."

"Well, you did. Good job." The Red Square set was magnificent. The first spot called for Sammy to do a dance routine with Speedy jumping onto his shoulder, then sliding down his arm to the ground, then the two of them doing a dance routine. All the while Sammy is lip-synching the music he recorded the night before. Now, instead of looking at the camera, he was directed to look down at Speedy during our duet. The camera then switched to a close-up of Speedy, who carried the melody. The melody we nailed down at 1:30 a.m.

To help Sammy visualize just where Speedy would be, they had little cutouts of the character and, during the rehearsals, placed them at key spots in the routine. It would be a month later before Speedy would be animated into the scene. So, Sammy had to react with Speedy by just imagining where he

157

would be.

It was something to see him prepare for his dance routine. He was such a quick study. He watched his stand-in go through the routine with the choreographer, then he jumped in and did it perfectly the first time. They were ready to shoot.

Then the most amazing scene took place. Sammy called in his bodyguard, who was carrying a locked briefcase. It was opened and Sammy took out another box. Out of that he removed an assortment of rings and other beautiful jewelry, which he put on. They shot the scene. By the third take they had it. Sammy called in the bodyguard, all the jewelry was removed, locked up tight, and they went on to rehearse the next scene. For the rest of the shoot, the same routine was repeated, time and time again. I don't know how many briefcases they wore out in a year.

At lunch with Mitch, I heard some exciting news. Miles was planning a nationwide tour, with me and Sammy, going to all Miles' major markets. We were to do all the talk shows and personal appearances they could line up. Our Winter Olympic spots had tested so well they were planning a whole new series to follow.

"When does your plane leave for the coast?"

"Four."

"OK. I have a photographer coming in to get some shots of you and Sammy."

The story took an even stranger twist. After speaking at a two-day motivational seminar in Canton, Ohio, and spending a week on the Michigan State campus, I flew 61Q to Elkhart to spend a day at Miles Laboratories in Indiana, about 100 miles east of Chicago. I asked Mitch how the tour was progressing.

"Fine, only we decided to send you, not Sammy. Can you handle it?"

"Yes, I've given it a lot of thought. I think it would be better that way. When are we going to do it?"

"Probably beginning in April. There are 14 markets. It will be quite a workout for you."

"I'll be ready."

After all that work preparing the difficult commercials in New York for the 1980 Summer Olympics, President Carter canceled our participation, and the spots were of no use.

In January, we met with a public relations firm, in their New York offices, to plan the tour. It was agreed, at my suggestion, that Speedy and the product be promoted, not Dick Beals.

"If they remember my name fine, but my job will be to promote product. I'll fly into each market in my airplane, which should get a lot of press. I'd like to speak to schoolchildren, and sign autographs, speak at universities, go on sales calls with the local Miles people, and push product.''

They agreed. To prepare, I wrote to all the Chamber of Commerce offices in the cities I would visit, and began memorizing everything I could.

Then the strangest twist of all occurred. Miles decided a new approach was needed in their commercials and Sammy's contract was not renewed. This also eliminated Speedy from their plans. The tour was canceled.

I was sorely disappointed. The only thing that helped me was the constant thought that everything works out for the best. As much as I thought it was just about the most perfect experience I could imagine, I concluded there must be something better. I read a phrase in a Unity booklet that said it best. It was almost as if it was talking to me. ''If it is right, right for you, right for everyone, it will move ahead. If it isn't, then it will not proceed; bless it, release it and move on to something better.''

A thought from long ago flashed into my mind. God knows what I want and where I belong. Do NOT tell God where the answers are. Know that you have already received the answer to your prayers, because . . . you have. God has worked out every detail. So, I ceased tying my future into what I thought was best. Instead, I focused on the goal, which was right there on my Golden Key list, 3. Voice-over work.

Once I got me out of the way, let go and let God do his work, things popped. During the Winter Olympics, an agent called me from Hollywood. He used to be with my long-time agent, Charles Stern. Now he was on his own.

''Dick, I've been watching your spots on the Winter Olympics. They're great.''

''Well, it helps when our hockey team beats Russia, doesn't it?''

''Are you considering coming back into the business?''

''Yes, Steve, I would very much like to be back. I realized during the Alka-Seltzer sessions how much I missed it. What do you think?''

''They are planning some big things at Hanna-Barbera. Have you talked to them lately?''

''Not for years.''

''Are you interested?''

''Sure, let's talk.''

Before I knew what was happening, I had auditioned for three new cartoon shows, won all three, and walked into another one. This meant a two-hour drive to Hollywood, 123 miles on the same freeways I left for quiet, peaceful Escondido.

In between the first recording session in New York with Sammy and my newfound career in Hollywood, the school board election reared its annoying head. Like a dummy, I allowed my name to be placed in nomination. The only reason I ran was because my campaign for increased discipline in the schools was so close to being adopted.

The teachers' union worked overtime to eliminate me from the board. They went door-to-door passing out literature for their candidates. They were also backing their candidates with a lot of money. By the time I discovered this, it was too late to take my name off the ballot, but when I saw the money they were spending to defeat me, I canceled all my advertising. I lost the election, but gratefully. The only disappointment was not being able to work with the young people.

At the next Rotary meeting, I was fined for losing the election, which got a big laugh. Sitting on one side of me was the new superintendent of the elementary school district, Don Hout, and on the other side, Frosty Fouts, the high school district superintendent. They didn't know whether to laugh or not, or quite what to say. Then Frosty chuckled, "Well, what are you going to do with all your spare time now, Dick?"

"I don't know, exactly. Do you know if any of your high school football coaches need any volunteer, part-time assistants?"

"Not offhand. But I can find out real quick. Are you interested?"

"Yes, as long as they understand my time constraints. I'd get a Pop Warner team, but I wouldn't have the time."

"You'll hear from me, one way or another."

I wasn't home 10 minutes, when the phone rang. It was Frosty. "Dick, your old friend, Coach Bob Woodhouse at San Pasqual tells me that the freshman coach could use some help. Are you interested?"

"That would be super. When and where?"

"You better hurry. Practice starts in 30 minutes. Meet Bob in his office and he'll introduce you to Joe Jayne." I wasn't much help at first to Coach Jayne because I didn't know their system or their techniques. I became a hand clapper, whistle tooter and giver-out of a lot of "attaboys." But to be involved in coaching again was heaven-sent.

The agency was doing well, I was flying 61Q to speaking engagements, and once again I was a busy actor. My prayers had been answered. And so it continued, year after year, with new challenges, new obstacles, new Golden Key lists. When the thoughts were positive, the results were positive. When I foolishly limited my thinking, the results were limited. When

I let go, and let God, and stayed out of the way, the results were like magic. Action was so swift and so sure and the results so good.

Even when the thought of semi-retirement flashed into my thinking, and I turned it over to a higher power, events occurred that were right for me, my business associates and my clients.

Daily freshman football and baseball coaching was replaced by football and basketball announcing. A desire to meet new people and a need for competition led me to duplicate bridge and traveling to tournaments all over the country.

I slowly eased out of the advertising business, and let Don carry on.

My work in Hollywood continued at a slower pace. But my prayers for voice-over work and a job as product spokesman were still on my Golden Key list.

The list was the basis for my meditation every day. It had never failed me yet. And it never would.

It had been 10 years since my exciting voice-over work with Alka-Seltzer and the Olympic commercials and the dream of the nationwide tour. I was reliving those wonderful moments when the phone rang.

"This is Dick Beals."

"Dick, this is Greg Decker, corporate communications, at Miles."

"Yes, sir, what can I do for you?"

"Well, we're planning a campaign to celebrate the 60th anniversary of Alka-Seltzer. We would like to involve you in our plans."

I couldn't believe what I was hearing. Trying to sound as businesslike as possible, I ventured forth with, "Sounds great. What do you want me to do?"

"Well, first of all, I understand from Don Yates that you're going to be back this way in two weeks. Would you be able to drop by here and attend a planning meeting?"

"Sure. I'll be on the Michigan State campus from October 6th to the 13th. I could drop by that week or before or after."

"It would have to be after, say, the 14th, because I'll be out of the country. If that's OK, then I'll ask our agency in New York to plan on that date, too."

"That will be fine. I'll be there."

"We can get together before the meeting and I'll bring you up to speed on our plans for you and get your input."

If my annual trip to the campus was exciting, the trip to Elkhart was even more so. I was placed in the Miles suite at the Ramada Inn, where Greg Decker reviewed the 60th

October 14, 1991, Dick signs the Guest
Register at the Miles Visitor Center in
Elkhart, Indiana. With him (left to right),
Dr. Don Yates, Roger Snow and Greg
Decker.

Dick with a Speedy doll, while the
original Speedy puppet, used in the
commercials, looks on.

His visit included autographing a
sizeable stack of Speedy photos.

Dick taped a 30 minute interview to be
beamed on satelite to TV stations all
over the country.

anniversary program. It was ambitious to say the least, but he had every angle covered.

The meeting the next day included the Alka-Seltzer product managers, Miles' historian, Dr. Don Yates, who also wrote their annual report and monthly newsletter, The Alkalizer, plus three representatives from GrossTownsend FrankHoffman, the New York public relations firm. They discussed and fine-tuned a most comprehensive program, to be launched with a December 4 press party in New York, featuring presentations by Don Yates and me, then a video salute to Alka-Seltzer's 60 glorious years.

The firm had radio and television talk-show interviews lined up for me. Even a lunch with Bob Costas, NBC's top sports personality.

The rest of the day included a lengthy taped interview reviewing my career as the voice of Speedy Alka-Seltzer, a tour of the Alka-Seltzer archives, and a goodly number of Speedy pictures to be autographed. The icing on the cake was being flown to Chicago in the Miles jet to catch my flight home.

The next seven weeks went by quickly, thank goodness, interspersed with numerous calls from Miles and GTFH. This was the most detail-oriented team I had ever encountered.

The New York trip finally arrived. Miles had a limo waiting for me at JFK. A team meeting was held upon my arrival to brief me on my schedule. The next day began with an Entertainment Tonight interview at 10 in a suite in the Grand Hyatt, where we were all headquartered.

Following that, it was out into the Big Apple's rain and gloom and into a waiting limo to be whisked off to our next talk show, then the meeting with Bob Costas.

He was in a production meeting when he spotted me. He jumped up, grabbed a baseball, opened the door, tossed me the ball and ran down the narrow hall, yelling, "Play Ball!" Unfortunately, my fastball knocked him out of his catcher's crouch and backward onto his wallet. Despite that he took me to the Broadway Grill for lunch.

This was truly an Angel Voice. I have never met a more dedicated, energetic, truthful, head-screwed-on-tight individual. He gave me a ton of ideas. He understood my life-long sports announcing dreams and my predicament of sports knowledge vs. childlike voice. I left sensing we would be conversing some more down the road.

Finally, all the planning, fine-tuning, checklists for checklists, rehearsals and last-minute critiques were behind us. The curtain was up, the spots were on, and the show began. M*A*S*H star, Larry Linville, known to millions as the goody-goody Major Burns, was the emcee. Don Yates gave us an

162

exquisite walk down memory lane. His conclusion was a real treat for me. He talked about my 40 years as a member of the Miles family and closed by presenting me with a gift, a colorful portrait of me and Speedy. It is a classic. In fact, it is my pleasure to share it with you. It is the cover on the book you are reading.

As emotional a moment as that was, there was work to do. The audience was applauding and it was now my turn. I reviewed the scary, early days in Hollywood, becoming Speedy, and described the contributions of the Speedy team including Miles President Charles Beardsley, Forrest Owen and Charles Chaplin. I sang some of my favorite commercials. Then I underscored that I was there that evening representing the larger Speedy team, a group of individuals who had accepted the challenge and delivered results. I closed by saying quite simply, "Miles . . . Speedy and I thank you."

The response was gratifying. The next hour was a blur of autographing Speedy pictures and posing for photos, beginning with the cake-cutting ceremony with Consumer Healthcare Division President Werner Spinner. Then came dozens of personal photo requests and chatting and shaking hands with our guests.

Exhausted? Never. This was the stuff dreams were made of. Best of all, this was just the beginning.

THINK BIGGER . . . .

December 3, 1991 — New York: Dick is invited to take part in Alka-Seltzer's 60th Anniversary celebration. He starts the day with an interview for the Entertainment Tonight television show.

Next a visit with NBC Sports' No. 1 man, Bob Costas, a long time Alka-Seltzer fan.

Dr. Don Yates, Dick and Consumer Healthcare Products' President Werner Spinner, prior to the 60th Anniversary media Kickoff Dinner.

Werner Spinner, President of Consumer Healthcare Products, presents Dick with a painting, in recognition of his 40 years with Alka-Seltzer.

In his presentation, Dick relates his 40 years as a member of the Alka-Seltzer team.

Werner Spinner and Dick cut the cake, with an assist from emcee Larry Linville, from the M.A.S.H. television show.